TABLE OF CONTENTS

1. Hosea's Family and God's Word 2

2. God's Wrath and Compassion 10

3. The Day of the Lord Is Near. 18

4. The Lord Roars From Zion. 27

5. Justice and Righteousness. 36

6. God's People Among the Nations 45

7. Judgment on Jerusalem 53

8. God's Peaceful Reign 61

9. God's Justice and Vengeance 69

10. The Reign of God 78

11. Visions of Restoration 87

12. God's Final Victory 96

13. The Messenger of the Lord 105

Hear the word of the LORD, you Israelites, /
because the LORD has a charge to bring / against you who live
in the land . . . (4:1).

— 1 —
Hosea's Family
and God's Word
Hosea 1–6

DIMENSION ONE:
WHAT DOES THE BIBLE SAY?

Answer these questions by reading Hosea 1

1. What is the Lord's first command to Hosea? (1:2)

2. Who is Hosea's wife? (1:3)

3. What does the Lord tell Hosea to name his first son, and why? (1:4)

4. What is the name of the prophet's daughter, and why? (1:6)

5. What does God tell Hosea to name his third child, and why? (1:9)

6. What will the people of Israel be called? (1:10)

Answer these questions by reading Hosea 2

7. What are the children to ask their mother to do? (2:2)

8. What did the wife not know? (2:8)

9. Who is speaking in Hosea 2:9-13? (2:13)

10. In the future, what will Israel (symbolized by the wife) say to the Lord? (2:16)

11. How will the Lord betroth Israel in the future? (2:19-20)

Answer these questions by reading Hosea 3

12. Why does the Lord command Hosea to love a woman who is an adulteress? (3:1)

13. Is the woman named? (3:1-5)

14. What will the children of Israel do afterward? (3:5)

Answer these questions by reading Hosea 4

15. Why does the Lord have a charge to bring against the inhabitants of the land? (4:1-2)

16. Who is addressed in Hosea 4:4-10? (4:4)

17. What do the people "consult," and what has led them astray? (4:12)

18. Who will be punished when the daughters turn to prostitution and the daughters-in-law commit adultery, and why? (4:14)

Answer these questions by reading Hosea 5

19. What does not permit the people of Ephraim to return to their God, and why? (5:4)

20. What is the Lord like to Ephraim and Judah? (5:12)

21. What did Ephraim do when he saw his sickness? (5:13)

22. What does the Lord expect the people to do? (5:15)

Answer these questions by reading Hosea 6

23. What does the Lord desire? (6:6)

24. What is the "horrible thing" in the house of Israel? (6:10)

DIMENSION TWO:
WHAT DOES THE BIBLE MEAN?

The Book of Hosea has two distinct parts. The first part is accounts and speeches concerning the family life of the prophet (Chapters 1–3). The second part is a series of prophetic speeches (Chapters 4–14). This lesson includes all of the first part and the beginning of the second.

The chapters about the prophet's family, though related to one another, are quite distinct. Chapter 1 is a third-person report about the Lord's command to Hosea and the prophet's fulfillment of the command. Hosea is to take an "adulterous wife" and have "children of unfaithfulness." Chapter 2 is a poetic form of a lawsuit against an unfaithful wife. Chapter 2 is connected to Chapter 1 by the names of the children. Chapter 3 is a first-person account by the prophet of the Lord's command to love a woman who is an adulteress. The speeches in Chapters 4–6 are mainly indictments or prophecies of punishment against the people of Israel. Some parts are addressed to specific groups of the people such as the priests.

❏ *Hosea 1:1.* Like most of the other prophetic books, this one begins with a superscription. This statement identifies the prophet and gives his dates in terms of the kings of Israel and Judah. It also says that the prophet's message is the revealed "word of the LORD."

❏ *Hosea 1:2.* The strange command for the prophet to take an adulterous wife introduces the main point of the first three chapters. The prophet's family life will present in a dramatic and powerful way a message concerning the relationship between the Lord and the people.

❏ *Hosea 1:4.* Prophets often were called by God to give their children symbolic names that embodied their messages. (See also Isaiah 7:14 and 8:1-3.) The name *Jezreel* and the expression *massacre at Jezreel* refer to the valley in Israel between Samaria and Galilee. These words also call to mind the story of the bloodshed there by Jehu. Jehu was Israel's ruler when Hosea began his work as a prophet (2 Kings 9–10).

❏ *Hosea 1:6-7.* The name *Lo-Ruhamah,* or "not loved," embodies an announcement of judgment against Israel. Judah, the Southern Kingdom, is not to be judged but delivered.

❏ *Hosea 1:9.* The name *Lo-Ammi,* or "not my people" presents the most devastating judgment possible. It alludes to the central expression of the covenant, "I will . . . be your God, and you will be my people" (Leviticus 26:12; see also Exodus 6:7; Deuteronomy 26:17-18). The Lord declares that the covenant relationship has ended.

❏ *Hosea 1:10-11.* These verses are an announcement of salvation. They promise that the judgment proclaimed through the name of the third child will not be the last word. One day the now-separate kingdoms of Judah and Israel will be united under a single king.

❏ *Hosea 2:2-15.* The prophet as husband brings a formal legal accusation against his unfaithful wife. The husband represents God and the wife symbolizes the people of Israel.

❑ *Hosea 2:8-9.* Israel's adultery involved the worship of Baal. The people failed to recognize that it is the Lord, and not Baal, who provides all good things.

❑ *Hosea 2:10-13.* The Lord will humiliate Israel before her lovers. God will lay waste to vines and fig trees, because the people worshiped Baal and forgot the Lord.

❑ *Hosea 2:14-18.* The Lord speaks of courting Israel, of a meeting in the desert, and of a tender relationship like a good marriage. Israel will be faithful like she was when the covenant was first established at the time of the Exodus. The new covenant will have cosmic dimensions, establishing peace among all living things.

❑ *Hosea 3.* This chapter reports a prophetic symbolic action. The Lord commands that the prophet act out the love of God for Israel in his own life. Israel will be deprived of leaders and of religious objects and practices in order to lead the people back to the Lord (verses 4-5).

❑ *Hosea 4:1-3.* The controversy (verse 1) is a lawsuit of the Lord against Israel. First the Lord calls the people to court (verse 1). Then God accuses Israel in terms of what the people have failed to do and what they have done. Then the Lord announces the punishment (verse 3).

❑ *Hosea 4:2.* The crimes or sins listed here correspond to five of the Ten Commandments (see Exodus 20:2-17; Deuteronomy 5:6-21). They are therefore violations of the specific laws long known to the people.

❑ *Hosea 4:6.* The priests will be punished because they have failed to perform one of their important duties, teaching the law of the Lord to the laity.

❑ *Hosea 4:12.* The "wooden idol" and the "stick of wood" refer to objects of worship or divination in Canaanite religion.

❑ *Hosea 4:13-14.* Verse 13 refers to common places of sacrifice and worship in the Canaanite fertility cult. The violations are not simply sexual promiscuity. They also include participation in cultic or religious prostitution.

❑ *Hosea 5:1-2.* Again Hosea addresses the priests. But here he includes other leaders who have led the people astray. *Snare, net,* and *slaughter* are hunting metaphors.

❑ *Hosea 5:6.* To seek the LORD is a technical expression that refers to a formal inquiry for the word of the Lord. Such inquiry will be futile. The Lord will punish Israel by withdrawing from the people.

❑ *Hosea 5:8.* The trumpet sound announces war. The places mentioned here are near the boundary between Israel and Judah. The following verses allude to the warfare of those two nations with one another.

❑ *Hosea 6:1-3.* Whether this prayer is a sincere expression of repentance or the prophet's satirical presentation of false and shallow religion is not clear.

Verse 2 does not refer to the resurrection of the people. The seriously wounded people express the confidence that they will be revived.

❑ *Hosea 6:6.* Mercy and acknowledgment of God are ideas central to the message of Hosea. They assume the covenant relationship with the Lord. These terms describe the proper human response, a trustworthy love and a knowledge that is deep and intimate.

DIMENSION THREE:
WHAT DOES THE BIBLE MEAN TO ME?

The Relationship Between God and People

The primary message of the Book of Hosea, and especially the first three chapters, concerns the intimate relationship between God and people. The prophet calls upon us to reflect on both sides of that relationship, the divine and the human. No other Old Testament book speaks more deeply of the nature and importance of the relationship between God and people, or of the disastrous results when the relationship is disrupted.

Hosea uses images and symbols to characterize God's relationship to Israel. Some of these images are the traditional language of covenant and election. But the new and distinctive images speak of love, marriage, children, and family. Are these images in any way disturbing? Is God's relationship to the people in any way like the relationship between a husband and a wife? If so, how?

If God's people behave like a prostitute or like an unfaithful wife, what is God to do? These chapters in Hosea present several answers to that question, from total judgment to redemption and salvation. Do you agree that the most drastic punishment is divorce, or for God to dissolve the relationship with the people (Hosea 1:9, 2:2)?

Read Romans 9:24-26. How does Paul reinterpret Hosea 1:10 and 2:23?

Faithfulness and Morality

Hosea says Israel's sin is prostitution. How is the prostitution of the people related to the other sins the prophet describes, for example in 4:2? What is the relationship between the failure to be faithful to God and injustice to one's neighbor? between religious practice and social responsibilities?

Hosea frequently describes faithfulness to the Lord as knowledge of God (2:20; 4:1, 6; 5:4; 6:6). What does the knowledge of God mean? Look at each verse listed. Note the terms that parallel it in the context. Discuss with the class the meaning and implications of this idea.

How can I give you up, Ephraim? / How can I hand you over, Israel? . . . all my compassion is aroused (11:8).

2
God's Wrath and Compassion
Hosea 7–14

DIMENSION ONE:
WHAT DOES THE BIBLE SAY?

Answer these questions by reading Hosea 7

1. When the Lord would heal Israel, what is exposed? (7:1)

2. How do the people delight the king and princes? (7:3)

3. Who calls upon the Lord? (7:7)

4. What testifies against Ephraim? (7:10)

5. What do the people do instead of crying out to the Lord from the heart? (7:14-16)

Answer these questions by reading Hosea 8

6. Why is an eagle (*vulture* in New Revised Standard Version) over the house of Israel? (8:1)

7. What will happen to the calf of Samaria? (8:6)

8. Why is Israel swallowed up and like a worthless thing? (8:8-9)

9. What is God about to do, and why? (8:13-14)

Answer these questions by reading Hosea 9

10. Where is Israel to go? (9:3)

11. How is the prophet characterized? (9:7-8)

12. Where did Israel become vile, and how? (9:10)

13. What will God do to the people of Israel, and why? (9:17)

Answer these questions by reading Hosea 10

14. How does Israel make promises and agreements? (10:4)

15. What will happen to the king in Samaria and to the high places of wickedness? (10:7-8)

16. What should Israel do, and why? (10:12)

Answer these questions by reading Hosea 11

17. Who is the speaker of the words recorded in Hosea 11:1-9?

18. How does God describe Israel, and what does that suggest about the nature of God? (11:1)

19. What did the Lord do for Ephraim? (11:3-4)

20. How are God's words in Hosea 11:8-9 different from those in Hosea 11:5-7?

21. Why will God not devastate Ephraim? (11:9)

Answer these questions by reading Hosea 12

22. What does it mean that Ephraim "feeds on the wind" and "pursues the east wind"? (12:1)

23. How does the Lord speak to and through the prophets? (12:10)

24. How did God bring Israel from Egypt? (12:13)

Answer these questions by reading Hosea 13

25. How does Ephraim sin more and more? (13:2)

26. What relationship does God have with Israel? (13:4-5)

27. What will happen to Samaria, and why? (13:16)

Answer these questions by reading Hosea 14

28. What does the prophet instruct the people to do? (14:1)

29. What is the person who is wise and discerning to do? (14:9)

DIMENSION TWO: WHAT DOES THE BIBLE MEAN?

Chapters 4–14 of the Book of Hosea are a collection of prophetic speeches. This lesson takes up the last part of the collection of speeches. Most of the addresses are presented as direct quotations of the Lord, though in others the prophet presents himself as the speaker. Most of the speeches are accusations against the people or prophecies of punishment. Some of the speeches announce salvation.

❏ *Hosea 7:1-2.* These two verses actually continue a speech that began either in Hosea 6:11b or 6:7. The Lord laments over Israel's action when God seeks to heal the people. *Heal* is one of Hosea's words for redemption. (See also Hosea 5:13 and 6:1.)

❏ *Hosea 7:3-7.* The theme of these verses is Israel's political life, and especially the sins and the coming end of the monarchy. The unidentified persons here ("their wickedness," "they are all adulterers") probably are not the people as a whole but political schemers and princes. The kings bring the trouble upon themselves because they do not call upon God.

❏ *Hosea 7:10.* The prophet describes Israel's sins. They have failed to return to and seek the Lord. Similar accusations occur in Hosea 7:7 and 7:14.

❏ *Hosea 7:11-12.* The image of a silly dove describes Israel's lack of faith in trying to make treaties with Egypt. The metaphor continues in the announcement of judgment: God will catch the birds in the nest.

❏ *Hosea 7:13-16.* These verses contain an announcement of punishment. Most of the speech spells out Israel's rebellion. This rebellion is in contrast to the Lord's gracious concern. The people have worshiped Baal. Judgment as destruction is introduced in verse 13 and announced specifically in verse 18.

Death will be by the sword and the people will be exiled to Egypt.

❑ *Hosea 8:1.* The law of God was given as a part of the covenant. See also Hosea 8:12.

❑ *Hosea 8:4-5.* Hosea often speaks unfavorably of the monarchy and not just against the sins of specific kings. He views the entire institution as corrupt and doomed.

❑ *Hosea 8:6.* The "calf of Samaria" is one of the two golden calves set up in the Northern Kingdom by its first ruler, Jeroboam. (See 1 Kings 12:28-29.)

❑ *Hosea 8:9-10.* Often Hosea uses the imagery of prostitution or adultery to describe Israel's worship of foreign gods such as Baal. Here he uses similar language to describe reliance upon treaties with foreign powers such as Assyria.

❑ *Hosea 8:11-14.* Does the Lord condemn all altars and sacrifices, or only their misuse? Hosea suggests that in his time all altars and sacrifices were corrupt.

❑ *Hosea 9:1-6.* With the direct address to the people, the prophet appears to interrupt a religious celebration. He is announcing that it will be Israel's last. He begins by commanding them to stop rejoicing (verse 1a). He then says Israel's unfaithfulness (verse 1b) is the reason for the bad news. The remainder of the speech (verses 2-6) announces their punishment. They will be exiled to Egypt and Assyria. This exile will bring to an end the religious celebrations they are enjoying as the prophet speaks.

❑ *Hosea 9:7-9.* As these verses continue the theme of judgment, they also give us two views of the prophet. The people view him as a fool and a maniac. They oppose him and hate him. But he sees himself as "the watchman over Ephraim."

❑ *Hosea 9:10-17.* Often in Hosea the period in the wilderness is seen as the time when the people of Israel were faithful to God. Here, though, it is described as the beginning of their worship of Baal.

❑ *Hosea 10:1-8.* Hosea links together two of Israel's sins, idolatrous worship and reliance upon a human king. The punishment corresponds to the crime.

❏ *Hosea 10:9-10*. The "days of Gibeah" may refer to the horrible event reported in Judges 19–21, the rape of the Levite's concubine and the subsequent warfare among the tribes of Israel.

❏ *Hosea 10:11-12*. Here Hosea uses farming metaphors. He contrasts the righteousness and unfailing love that God expects of Israel (verse 12) with the wickedness, evil, and deception (verse 13) that characterize their lives.

❏ *Hosea 10:13-15*. This speech of the prophet has two parts. The first part is the accusation or reasons for punishment (verse 13). The second part is the announcement of punishment (verses 14-15). The point is clear: those who live by the chariot die by the chariot.

❏ *Hosea 11:1-12*. This entire speech (except verse 10) is a divine meditation on Israel's future. God agonizes over the fact that the more Israel was treated like a young son, the more that son rebelled (verses 1-4). So the Lord vows to punish that rebellion with a return to Egypt, an exile in Assyria, and a total military defeat (verses 4-7). But then God's compassion wins out over wrath (verses 8-9). If the Lord decided Israel's future by the scales of human justice, punishment would be justified. But God's mercy transcends human justice (verse 9).

❏ *Hosea 12:2-6*. As in Hosea 4:1-3, the Lord brings Israel into court. The indictment (verses 2-4) consists of a recital of the deeds of Jacob, the ancestor of the people, as reported in the Book of Genesis.

❏ *Hosea 12:10-14*. The Lord is responsible for prophetic visions and sayings. God even used a prophet (Moses) to bring Israel out of Egypt (verse 13).

❏ *Hosea 13:1-3*. God indicts the people (Ephraim) for idolatry and false worship. God announces judgment on them. The announcement uses four similes (morning mist, dew, chaff, smoke) to say that Israel will disappear.

❏ *Hosea 13:4-16*. After recalling how Israel was delivered from Egypt, cared for in the desert, and given a rich land (verses 4-6a), the Lord notes that the people forgot God (verse 6b). God promises, at length and in detail, to turn against them (verses 7-16).

16   THE MINOR PROPHETS

❏ *Hosea 14:4-8.* These words appear as the divine answer to the prayer of the people. The Lord promises to heal even the faithlessness of the people and to make them flourish and prosper.

❏ *Hosea 14:9.* These words recommend the book to its readers as a way to learn and follow the "ways of the LORD."

DIMENSION THREE:
WHAT DOES THE BIBLE MEAN TO ME?

Judgment or Salvation?

Explore the question of the relationship between God's wrath and mercy. First decide whether the issue is resolved in the Book of Hosea. According to Hosea, what is God's last word for Israel, one of judgment or one of salvation? From the beginning of the book to its end, there are far more words of accusation and announcements of punishment than of salvation. Israel has sinned, primarily by turning to false gods but also by acts of injustice. Because of this sin the people deserve to be punished. God will bring about their defeat and destruction. But some parts of the book suggest a different outcome. The punishment might be temporary. Or it might bring repentance and true faithfulness. First judgment, then, salvation. But other passages, especially Chapter 11, go even beyond that. God's wrath and love struggle with each other, and love wins out.

From the point of view of the New Testament and the Christian faith, the question has a clear answer. God's last word is the good news of love and salvation. But, as the Book of Hosea shows, men and women of faith wrestled with the problem long before the time of Jesus. Some persons even had a vision of divine mercy that holds back wrath and takes the initiative to save a sinful people.

Is there room in our Christian faith for the idea of judgment? According to Paul, the law and prophets still witness to God's righteousness (Romans 3:21). Presumably the law and prophets also witness to God's condemnation of injustice and unfaithfulness. Will those who sow the wind reap the whirlwind (Hosea 8:7)?

*Your sons and your daughters will prophesy, / your old men
will dream dreams, / your young men will see visions (2:28).*

— 3 —
The Day of the Lord
Is Near
Joel 1–3

DIMENSION ONE:
WHAT DOES THE BIBLE SAY?

Answer these questions by reading Joel 1

1. How is the Book of Joel introduced and defined? (1:1)

2. What insects have attacked the land and its crops? (1:4)

3. How is the nation that has invaded the land described?
   (1:6)

4. Why does Joel call for the people to mourn? (1:8-10)

5. Why are the priests called to put on sackcloth and mourn? (1:13)

6. What should the priests and the people do? (1:14)

7. What will the day of the Lord be like? (1:15-16)

Answer these questions by reading Joel 2

8. What will happen when the day of the Lord is coming? (2:1)

9. How does the prophet describe the enemy? (2:4-5)

10. Whose army is it that causes the earth to shake and the sun and moon to be darkened? (2:10-11)

11. What does the Lord want the people to do? (2:12-13)

12. Why should the people return to their God? (2:13-14)

THE DAY OF THE LORD IS NEAR

13. Who should come to the sacred assembly? (2:16)

14. Why do the priests think God should spare the people? (2:17)

15. What does the Lord say to the land, the wild animals, and the people of Zion? (2:21-23)

16. What is the great army that the Lord had sent among the people? (2:25)

17. What are the people to know? (2:27)

18. What are the results when the Lord's Spirit is poured out on all people? (2:28-29)

19. What are the wonders in the heavens and on the earth? (2:30-31)

Answer these questions by reading Joel 3

20. What does the Lord promise to do to Judah and Jerusalem? (3:1-2)

THE MINOR PROPHETS

21. What is the Lord's accusation against Tyre, Sidon, and all the regions of Philistia? (3:5-6)

22. When war is proclaimed among the nations, what are the people to do? (3:10)

23. What is the day of the Lord near? (3:14)

24. What is to happen to Egypt and Edom? to Judah and Jerusalem? (3:19-20)

DIMENSION TWO:
WHAT DOES THE BIBLE MEAN?

The Book of Joel is a report of a prophetic liturgy in two parts. The first part (Joel 1:2–2:17) includes the prophet's directions to the community to convene a service of complaint and petition to God. One reason they should do this is because of the threat of a plague of locusts (1:4-20). Another reason is because of the danger of the day of the Lord. The second part of the book (Joel 2:18–3:21) reports the Lord's responses to genuine repentance. God promises salvation and assures the people that they have been heard. The danger from the locusts has evoked the fear of a cosmic day of the Lord. In the end, the day of the Lord will be turned into a day of salvation because the people have trusted in the compassion of their God.

❏ *Joel 1:1.* This superscription is like most others that begin prophetic books. By characterizing what follows as "the word of the LORD," this verse asserts that the book is a revelation from God. Unlike many superscriptions to prophetic books, however, this one gives no indication of the date of the prophet. Joel quotes the words of several earlier prophets. For this reason, and because of the historical and social situation that the book assumes, Joel usually is dated in the fifth or fourth century B.C.

❑ *Joel 1:2-3.* The prophet begins with a summons to all the people to hear of a great event and pass the report on down through the generations. That event is the locust plague. The plague is taken as a sign that the day of the Lord is near (Joel 1:15). The "elders" were the leaders of the community.

❑ *Joel 1:4.* This verse is the keynote of the first part of the Book of Joel. It emphasizes the total destruction in the wake of the locust invasion. The different kinds of locusts may refer to developmental stages of one kind of insect.

❑ *Joel 1:5-14.* This unit is a long and complicated call to worship. Joel clearly speaks as a prophet, quoting the words of the Lord in verses 6 and 7. He also speaks as a leader in worship, a role more commonly associated with priests. The focus of attention is not on the locusts themselves but on the results of their invasion, destruction that is the occasion for prayer.

❑ *Joel 1:5-7.* All those who drink wine are called to mourn because the wine is gone. The nation that has attacked is the horde of locusts that has cut down the vines.

❑ *Joel 1:8-10.* Israel's mourning, says Joel, should be like that of a young bride for her husband who has died. The priests and ministers mourn because there is no grain or drink for the offerings in the Temple. All the produce of the ground is lost.

❑ *Joel 1:11-12.* Now the farmers and those who work the vineyards are called to cry out. The harvest has been devastated, and the plants themselves are dying. As a result, all joy has disappeared.

❑ *Joel 1:13.* The prophet repeats his call to the priests and ministers to mourn. They should put on sackcloth and cry because there is nothing to offer to God in the Temple.

❑ *Joel 1:14.* In a summary of the entire passage, Joel instructs the priests to proclaim a fast and a service of mourning. They should call everyone to the Temple and "cry out to the LORD."

The prayer service will include mourning and a petition to the Lord for help.

❑ *Joel 1:15-16.* With a cry of terror, Joel introduces the central theme of the book. The theme is about the approach of the day of the Lord. The coming day of the Lord is well known in both earlier and later biblical literature. This day was seen as a fearful occasion when the Lord will come to destroy the enemies and establish kingship over the world. Those enemies may be the people of Israel themselves (Amos 5:18-20) or the other nations. Joel sees the destruction in the wake of the locust plague as a sign that the day of the Lord is drawing near.

❑ *Joel 1:17-18.* Often prayers of complaint and lamentation describe the trouble that has occasioned the prayers.

❑ *Joel 1:19-20.* The description of disaster continues. In the form of direct address to God, it follows an invocation of the Lord's name. The prophet tells God the destruction is so bad that even the wild animals pray to the Lord.

❑ *Joel 2:1-11.* With terror in his voice, the prophet issues a call to sound the alarm in Jerusalem. The reason for his cry and fear is given both at the beginning and the end: "the day of the LORD is coming" (verse 1), and it is "great" and "dreadful" (verse 11). The remainder of the section (verses 2b-10) is a vivid description of an approaching army. Is this army the locust plague of Chapter 1? or yet another invasion of locusts? More likely, Joel refers to the terrible warfare on the day of the Lord. This day is known from earlier prophetic texts and echoes in later apocalyptic visions of the end. Such images form the background for the great battle at Armageddon at the end time (Revelation 16:16).

❑ *Joel 2:3-5.* The army with its chariots turns the land from a paradise into a desert.

❑ *Joel 2:6-9.* As a well-disciplined army moves forward and into the city it terrifies the people.

❑ *Joel 2:10-11.* The army even brings dramatic cosmic effects. It causes the earth to quake and the heavens to tremble. The sun, the moon, and the stars all darken.

❑ *Joel 2:12-14.* Two calls for repentance are uttered. In the first (verses 12-13a), the Lord speaks. In the second (verses 13b-14), the prophet addresses the people. Both speeches call for a sincere return to the Lord. The people must trust in God's grace, mercy, and unfailing love. The people should be enabled to repent, for their God is one who "relents from sending calamity." (See Hosea 11:8-9.)

❏ *Joel 2:15-17.* Joel directs the priests to call the people to a service of prayer. He instructs them in the prayer of petition (verse 17), the heart of the service.

❏ *Joel 2:18-32.* Beginning with Joel 2:18, the form, tone, and content of the book change to describe the Lord's response to the repentant people. Following the report that God was aroused for the land and had pity on the people, the prophet presents a series of oracles of assurance, salvation, and hope.

❏ *Joel 2:19-20.* The Lord promises to restore the produce of the land and to drive the enemy away.

❏ *Joel 2:21-24.* With words of assurance, Joel sings a hymn of praise to God for the blessings of nature.

❏ *Joel 2:25-27.* Again God speaks promising salvation to Israel. When all needs are fulfilled, the people will know that God is in their midst, and there is no other God.

❏ *Joel 2:28-29.* God promises a gift beyond material goods. One day the Spirit of the Lord will be poured out on "all people."

❏ *Joel 2:30-32.* In language that echoes Joel 2:10, the Lord announces the signs of the day of the Lord. But terrible and terrifying as it will be, "everyone who calls on the name of the LORD will be saved."

❏ *Joel 3:1-21.* While these oracles continue to announce salvation to Israel, their dominant feature is the announcement of judgment on foreign nations.

❏ *Joel 3:1-8.* When the Lord restores the fortunes of Judah and Jerusalem, God will call the nations to judgment because of their injustice to the people of God. The Philistines in particular are singled out for punishment.

❏ *Joel 3:9-15.* God announces that the day of the Lord will be a time of holy war against the nations. Contrast these verses with the promise of eternal peace found in Isaiah 2:4 and Micah 4:3.

❏ *Joel 3:16-21.* The Lord promises to protect Jerusalem and make it a safe place for the people of Israel. Egypt and Edom will be destroyed because of their injustice (verse 18). The people of God will inhabit a rich and fruitful land (verse 18) for all generations.

DIMENSION THREE:
WHAT DOES THE BIBLE MEAN TO ME?

The Day of the Lord

The threat and promise of the day of the Lord, as presented in Joel, pose questions for Christians. The prophet himself had inherited from earlier prophets and Scriptures the same question that is before us: Will God come to judge and destroy or to restore and save? The words of God handed down to Joel about the day of the Lord contained both threats and promises. But often they saw the day in terms of war against the enemies of God. Joel understands the locust plague as a harbinger of that fateful day and as threatening to Israel. But the Lord will eventually fight against the other nations and come to dwell on Zion with the people. Is that view too narrow in the light of the New Testament?

The Old Testament itself presents us with more than one view of God's coming actions. To see the contrasts between such views, read Joel 3:9-10 and then read Isaiah 2:4 and Micah 4:3. Isaiah and Micah have a vision of eternal peace, in which all nations participate. Joel reverses the very language of that vision, seeing salvation for the people of Israel in the military defeat of their enemies. How can these expectations be reconciled with each other?

The Relationship of Repentance to Salvation

The salvation of the people of God in Joel is seen to occur in history and on the earth. It will entail peace following the terrible day of the Lord, and nature that will become fruitful and supportive. Is that view too materialistic for Christians? Has it been superseded by hope of salvation beyond time and the world? Certainly Christians need to consider such promises in the light of the New Testament, but they should not be rejected too quickly. Is not the kingdom of God that time and place where God's will reigns, both in this world and the next? Does not God will that people live in peace and that the hungry be fed?

The words of Joel turn from judgment to hope and salvation as soon as the people express their genuine repentance to God. On the surface it might appear that they saved themselves by saying the right prayers, by the sincerity of their repentance. But not so, for two reasons. First, the salvation of the people rests not on saying the right prayers, but on their trust in God's compassion and in the eventual triumph of that compassionate God. Paul's understanding of faith as trust in God (see Romans 2–3) is like this view. Salvation is presented as the free initiative and gift of God, which cannot and need not be earned.

You only have I chosen / of all the families of the earth; /
therefore I will punish you / for all your sins (3:2).

—— 4 ——
The Lord Roars From Zion
Amos 1–4

DIMENSION ONE:
WHAT DOES THE BIBLE SAY?

Answer these questions by reading Amos 1

1. When did Amos see his words concerning Israel? (1:1)

2. What happens when the Lord roars from Zion and thunders from Jerusalem? (1:2)

3. Why does the Lord refuse to revoke the punishment of Damascus? (1:3)

4. What will happen when the Lord breaks down the gate of Damascus and destroys the king of the Valley of Aven and the one who holds the scepter from Beth Eden? (1:5)

5. Why will the Lord send fire to destroy the walls and the fortresses of Gaza? (1:6-7)

6. What are the sins of Tyre? (1:9)

7. Why does the Lord refuse to revoke the punishment of the Ammonites? (1:13)

Answer these questions by reading Amos 2

8. Why does the Lord refuse to revoke the punishment of Judah? (2:4)

9. How does Israel treat the righteous, the needy, the poor, and the oppressed? (2:6-7)

10. What does Israel do in the house of God? (2:8)

11. What has the Lord done for the people of Israel? (2:9-11)

12. What are the people of Israel accused of doing to the Nazirites and the prophets? (2:12)

13. When the Lord judges Israel, what will happen to the swift, the strong, and the warrior? (2:14)

Answer these questions by reading Amos 3

14. Why will the Lord punish Israel for all its sins? (3:2)

15. What does the Lord do without revealing his plan to the prophets? (3:7)

16. What is happening in Samaria? (3:9-10)

17. What houses does the Lord promise to destroy on the day of Israel's punishment? (3:15)

Answer these questions by reading Amos 4

18. What does the Lord swear to do to the "cows of Bashan"? (4:1-3)

19. What do the people of Israel love to do when they come to Bethel and Gilgal? (4:4-5)

20. What is the refrain that recurs five times in Amos 4:6-11?

21. What did the Lord withhold when there were just three months to the harvest? (4:7)

22. When the Lord overthrew some as when Sodom and Gomorrah were overthrown, what was Israel like? (4:11)

23. What does the Lord call for Israel to do? (4:12)

24. Who forms the mountains and creates the wind? (4:13)

DIMENSION TWO:
WHAT DOES THE BIBLE MEAN?

The Book of Amos consists primarily of short prophetic speeches. It also contains reports of the prophet's visions, the account of one event in the prophet's life, and three short hymns or fragments of hymns (Amos 4:13; 5:8-9; 9:5-6). The book has two major sections. Chapters 1–6 contain speeches, and Chapters 7–9 are organized around five vision reports. Chapters 1–4, the focus of this lesson, include the superscription and motto of the book (Amos 1:1-2), a series of prophecies against foreign nations culminating in a prophecy against Israel (Amos 1:3–2:16), and a series of prophecies against Israel (Amos 3:1–4:13).

The message of the prophet is clear and strong. The Lord will punish the people of Israel with a total military disaster because of their social injustice and religious arrogance.

□ *Amos 1:1.* This superscription contains more information about the book and the prophet than that of any other prophetic book. Amos is identified as a shepherd. He is from the little town of Tekoa, south of Bethlehem (and thus in Judah). He came north to the country of Israel to speak what God had called him to say. The date of the earthquake mentioned here is not known. But judging by the dates of the two kings, the activity of Amos can be dated to approximately 760 B.C.

□ *Amos 1:2.* This verse serves as a general statement about the message of the prophet. It could serve as a motto to the book as a whole. The word of the Lord, through the southern prophet, comes from Jerusalem and is directed to the north, epitomized by Mount Carmel.

□ *Amos 1:3–2:16.* This long section of the book is designed to be read or heard as a whole. The section is a series of eight prophecies in two parts. The first part contains seven addresses against foreign nations. The second part is a prophecy against Israel.

Readers of the book often have taken the seven speeches against the foreign nations primarily as rhetorical preparation for the prophecy against Israel. The listeners agree with everything the prophet says against the enemies. Suddenly he turns on them. The goal of the series is obviously the last speech against Israel. The emphasis usually falls on the last element in a series. And this speech is the longest and most detailed statement of both crimes and punishment. However, we should not read the other speeches simply as rhetorical flourishes. They must have been meant no less seriously than the final speech. Amos understands that the Lord of Israel and Judah also holds all nations accountable for justice and righteousness. God's authority is not limited by national boundaries.

□ *Amos 1:3-5.* This prophecy, like the others in the series, has two main parts. The first part is a statement of crimes (or transgressions or sins) as reasons for punishment (verse 3). The second part is the announcement of punishment (verses

4-5). The speech begins and ends with formulas that identify the words as direct quotations of the Lord.

Damascus was the capital of Syria (verse 5). In the past Syria had been both an enemy and an ally of Israel. Its crime was harsh treatment of Gilead. Gilead was a city in the Transjordan. Here the name probably stands for an entire section of Israel. A destruction by fire is announced on the royal household, the fortresses of the king. The people will go into exile.

❏ *Amos 1:6-8.* This prophecy concerns the Philistines. It begins as an address concerning Gaza. Eventually it lists other Philistine cities (Ashdod, Ashkelon, and Ekron). Finally it promises that God's wrath will continue until "the last of the Philistines is dead" (verse 8).

❏ *Amos 1:9-10.* Tyre was the leading trade and shipping center of Phoenicia. Elsewhere in the Old Testament, Solomon made a treaty with Hiram, the king of Tyre. Hiram provided timber and artisans for the construction of the Temple in Jerusalem (1 Kings 5). Tyre's transgression included the violation of a treaty, called "a treaty of brotherhood" (verse 9).

❏ *Amos 1:11-12.* Edom's "brother" here is probably the country of Judah. Old Testament tradition recalls that the Edomites and the Israelites had common ancestors. The relations between the two peoples seldom were good after the time of David. Animosity becomes especially strong in the time of the Babylonian Exile and afterwards.

❏ *Amos 1:13-14.* The Ammonites, who like the Edomites lived east of the Jordan, are accused of brutal acts during a war of aggression. The war was against their northern neighbors in Gilead.

❏ *Amos 2:1-3.* That Moab "burned, as if to lime, / the bones of Edom's king," is itself bad enough. Even an enemy as hated as Jezebel (2 Kings 9:34) deserves a proper burial. But this act must stand as well for other crimes, such as war against Edom, and killing its king.

❏ *Amos 2:4-5.* Judah's punishment is the same as all the other nations. Her transgressions, however, are quite different. The other nations have violated generally accepted principles for relationships among nations. Judah is held accountable to "the law of the Lord and . . . his decrees." In one sense this accusa-

32   THE MINOR PROPHETS

tion is more narrow than the others because it is based on the revealed will of God. But in another sense it is broader since no specific crimes are listed.

❏ *Amos 2:6-16.* The accusations against Israel are both specific and concrete. The prophet is speaking for the Lord. He lists a series of injustices against the poor and the weak (verses 6-8). He then reminds the people of the great acts of the Lord for Israel. The great acts include the Exodus, the giving of the land, and the election of some as prophets and Nazirites (verses 9-11). After making further accusations (verse 12), the Lord promises intervention with violence against Israel (verses 13-16).

❏ *Amos 3:1-2.* This speech is a key to understanding the Book of Amos. The speech is a summary of a major aspect of the prophet's message. Amos reminds the people of Israel, as in 2:9-10, that the Lord chose them and brought them out of Egypt. For this reason, God will punish them for their iniquities. Election has become a terrifying thing because of the special responsibilities it entails. These verses epitomize the idea that of those to whom much is given, much will be required.

❏ *Amos 3:3-8.* This speech is a series of proverbial sayings. Each saying makes the point that every cause has its effect and every effect its cause (verses 3-6). Verse 7 is a general statement about the way God acts. Verse 8 applies the principle of cause and effect to the activity of prophets. Prophecy is the effect of a divine cause.

❏ *Amos 3:9-11.* Foreigners are called to observe all the violence and oppression in Samaria, the capital of Israel. Because of that violence, an enemy will invade the land and overcome the fortresses.

❏ *Amos 4:1-3.* This prophecy of punishment is addressed to the wealthy women of the capital city. They are ridiculed as "cows of Bashan." Guilty of two kinds of sin, social injustice and arrogance, they are epitomized by what they say to their husbands.

❏ *Amos 4:4-5.* This speech is rich with irony. Calls to worship have become accusations of transgressions.

❏ *Amos 4:6-12.* The refrain, "yet you have not returned to me," becomes an interpretation of a series of catastrophes and an indictment of the people. God sought to bring Israel to her senses through famine (verse 6), drought (verses 7-8), loss of crops (verse 9), pestilence (verse 10), and military losses (verse 11). The people did not respond. Consequently, their time is now up and they should prepare to meet an obviously angry God (verse 12).

❏ *Amos 4:13.* This is the first of three similar hymnlike passages in Amos. These passages extol the greatness and power of God (Amos 5:8-9 and 9:5-6).

DIMENSION THREE:
WHAT DOES THE BIBLE MEAN TO ME?

The Meaning of Election

Amos and his original audience assumed that God had chosen Israel to be the people of God. That election fulfilled promises made to the patriarchs, carried out through the Exodus and the granting of the land of Canaan, and continued through God's care for the people.

Amos, however, qualifies the ancient belief in two ways. On the one hand, he emphasizes that election entails special responsibilities (Amos 3:1-12) to the point that election has become a terrifying thing. But, the prophet also knows that God's concern and authority extend far beyond the chosen people, both in positive and negative terms. On the positive side, he reports that the God who brought Israel out of Egypt also brought other nations to their lands (Amos 9:7-8). And on the negative side he hears the Lord announcing judgment upon other nations as well as Israel (Amos 1:3–2:3). Israel is special, to be sure, but God's concern and justice know no boundaries.

Our nation's Pilgrim ancestors saw themselves as God's elect, entering and establishing a new promised land. Do we, as Christians and Americans, view ourselves as God's chosen people? If so, how does the prophet Amos challenge our understanding of ourselves?

God's Judgment

One of the most difficult themes of the Old Testament prophets is the central message of the Book of Amos—the announcement that God is about to judge the people by bringing total military disaster. This message seems to embody a God of wrath and vengeance. This description of God is one of the most awkward for Christians. Certainly for Christians the last word must be found in the New Testament, where the nature of God is revealed through Jesus Christ. Is the message of Amos—that God acts against injustice—any longer valid? How?

Does the New Testament insist that the God revealed in and through Jesus Christ is the same God who chose and loved and judged ancient Israel? According to the Bible, is God's justice contrary to God's love? Does evil behavior always lead to bad consequences? Do the Old Testament writers always agree about the limits of divine retribution? Many sayings in Proverbs, for example, see a direct relationship between a person's goodness and well-being. What does Job say about why the righteous suffer?

*Let justice roll on like a river, /
righteousness like a never-failing stream (5:24).*

—— 5 ——
Justice and Righteousness
Amos 5–9

DIMENSION ONE:
WHAT DOES THE BIBLE SAY?

Answer these questions by reading Amos 5

1. How does Amos identify the "word"? (5:1)

2. What will happen to the city that marches out a thousand and the town that marches out a hundred? (5:3)

3. What does the Lord call for Israel to do? (5:4-5)

4. Whose sins are great? (5:12)

5. What will the day of the Lord be like? (5:18-20)

6. How does the Lord feel about Israel's religious feasts, assemblies, offerings, and songs? (5:21-23)

7. What does God want to happen instead of feasts? (5:24)

Answer these questions by reading Amos 6

8. To whom does Amos address his cry of woe? (6:1)

9. What is to happen to those who live in luxury? (6:4-7)

10. What have the people done to justice and the fruit of righteousness? (6:12)

Answer these questions by reading Amos 7

11. What did Amos do after his vision of locusts eating up the crops? (7:1-3)

12. What did God do after Amos's vision of judgment by fire? (7:4-6)

13. How does the Lord explain the meaning of the vision of the plumb line to the prophet? (7:7-9)

14. Of what does Amaziah accuse Amos? (7:10-11)

15. Why does Amaziah prohibit Amos from prophesying at Bethel? (7:13)

16. Why does Amos speak against Israel? (7:14-15)

17. Why will Amaziah and his family be punished? (7:16-17)

Answer these questions by reading Amos 8

18. What vision is the occasion for announcing that the end has come upon the people of Israel? (8:1-3)

19. What do those who trample the needy and do away with the poor of the land say? (8:4-6)

20. What will the Lord do "in that day"? (8:9-10)

21. What kind of famine will there be in the days ahead? (8:11-12)

Answer these questions by reading Amos 9

22. Who will escape the judgment of the Lord? (9:1)

23. What will the Lord do to those who hide at the bottom of the sea? (9:3)

24. In addition to bringing Israel up from Egypt, who else did the Lord bring up, and from where? (9:7)

25. What will happen to all the sinners among God's people? (9:10)

26. What will the Lord do to David's fallen tent? (9:11)

27. What does the Lord promise to do concerning the fortunes of the people of Israel? (9:14)

DIMENSION TWO:
WHAT DOES THE BIBLE MEAN?

Chapters 5–9 are the focus of this lesson. They include the last part of the collection of prophetic speeches and the entire second section of traditions organized around the five vision reports. Between the third and fourth vision reports is a story of a conflict between Amos and Amaziah. Amaziah was the priest of Bethel (7:10-17). The visions, like virtually all the speeches of Amos, announce that the Lord is about to intervene in history. God will judge the nation of Israel through a total military disaster because of her sins. She is especially guilty of social injustice and religious arrogance.

❏ *Amos 5:1-2.* This short speech begins with the prophet's call to hear. A similar expression begins several addresses (3:1; 4:1). The "word" that Amos has to proclaim is identified as a lament or dirge. The nation is as good as dead.

❏ *Amos 5:3.* The prophet's purpose is not to reassure the people that some remnant will be left over from the coming disaster. He is emphasizing how complete the judgment will be. The verse does not indicate that the ten percent who might survive will be chosen on the basis of their goodness.

❏ *Amos 5:4-7.* In these verses we find some of the prophet's rare exhortations to the people to change their ways before it is too late. Seeking the Lord leads to life. Those who corrupt justice and reject righteousness (verse 7) are addressed here. Seeking the Lord corresponds to establishing justice and righteousness. (See also Amos 5:14-15.)

❏ *Amos 5:8-9.* Like many of the psalms, this hymn extols the Lord as the creator of the cosmos. God made the constellations, causes day and night, and brings the rain from the sea. The Lord is also the name of the one who can intervene in history to destroy.

❏ *Amos 5:10-13.* The word translated in the NRSV as *they* in verse 10 refers to the same persons addressed as *you* in verses 11 and 12, and is translated that way in the NIV. They are the ones who have the power to "trample on the poor," "oppress the righteous," "take bribes," and "deprive the poor of justice in the courts." They also have built fine houses and planted vineyards. Consequently, the words of Amos here are directed to the wealthy and powerful members of the community. They misuse their power and deprive the poor of their rights.

❏ *Amos 5:16-17.* This passage is similar to Amos 5:1-2 in that it announces judgment upon Israel. It describes the mourning that will follow the coming disaster.

❏ *Amos 5:18-20.* This reference to the expectation of the day of the Lord is the earliest of the prophetic references to such a day. Amos clearly means to correct a false idea held by his hearers. They see that day as one of salvation. Amos says it will bring judgment.

❏ *Amos 5:21-27.* Here the prophet has the Lord rejecting all kinds of religious practices and observances. God calls instead for justice and righteousness. Does Amos mean that all worship services, sacrifices, and hymns should be stopped? Or does he mean that worship without the practice of justice and righteousness is corrupt?

❏ *Amos 6:1-7.* This address also begins with the cry of "woe." It criticizes the wealthy for their arrogance and self-satisfaction. The final word is that they will be the first to go into exile (verse 7).

❏ *Amos 6:8-14.* The theme that holds these verses together is the destruction of Israel. The city mentioned in verse 8 is probably the capital city of Samaria.

❏ *Amos 7:1-9.* Amos, like most of the other prophets, could present his message by reporting his visionary experiences. Three of his five vision reports occur here in this chapter. The fourth is in Amos 8:1-3 and the fifth in 9:1-4. The first two reports (verses 1-3 and 4-6) are identical in form. Amos reports that God showed him the vision of a threatening thing (locusts, judgment by fire). He then prayed for Jacob, and the Lord repented, deciding not to carry out the destruction. The third and fourth reports (7:7-9 and 8:1-3) likewise are similar to each other. The vision shown by God is not of a threatening thing. But in the conversation between the Lord and the prophet it becomes the basis for announcing God's judgment.

❏ *Amos 7:10-17.* The account of the encounter between Amos and Amaziah the priest of Bethel is a story of conflict. The conflict is between the prophet and the established religious and political authorities. Amaziah commands Amos to return to Judah, for he has no authority in Bethel, a royal sanctuary in Israel. Amos first responds to the question of his authority to speak. He then announced judgment upon Amaziah for attempting to stand in the way of the word of God. Amos rests his case not on whether or not he is or was a prophet, but upon his call. He has the right, indeed the responsibility, to speak the word of God to Israel because God commanded him to do so.

❑ *Amos 8:1-3.* The fourth vision report, like the third vision report (7:7-9), conveys a message of judgment upon Israel.

❑ *Amos 9:1-4.* The fifth and final vision is the most radical of all. The prophet sees God over the altar commanding that the "tops of the pillars" of the Temple be shattered on the people. Those who escape will die by the sword. Furthermore, none can escape from the judgment. They cannot escape in heaven, nor on earth (represented by Mount Carmel), nor in the bottom of the sea, nor in captivity. The judgment on the people will be total and uncompromising.

❑ *Amos 9:5-6.* Like Amos 4:13 and 5:8-9, this passage is a fragment of a hymn in praise of the Lord's majesty and creative work.

❑ *Amos 9:7-8.* These verses contain some of the most remarkable lines in all of the early prophetic books. To God, Israel and the Ethiopians are the same. To be sure, says Amos, the Lord elected Israel by bringing the people out of Egypt. But God also brought the Philistines from Caphtor and the Arameans from Kir. Election will not save Israel from judgment.

❑ *Amos 9:9-15.* The final verses of the book are quite unlike the other words attributed to Amos. Quite possibly they were added centuries later. While Amos sees judgment coming on the entire people, verses 9-10 restrict it to certain sinners. While Amos sees only disaster, verses 11-15 assume that the land is destroyed and the people are in exile. The verses look beyond to a time of restoration. By seeing that God had a new and bright future in store for the people, the later voices did not deny the truth of the prophet's words of judgment. To the contrary, they read the announcements of Amos from an earlier time and applied them to themselves. Amos was right.

God punished us through the Exile, and now God is acting to restore.

DIMENSION THREE:
WHAT DOES THE BIBLE MEAN TO ME?

Amos 5:10-15, 21-24; 8:4-6—Justice and Righteousness

One of the most powerful themes in the Book of Amos is the accusation that the people have corrupted justice and righteousness. What do the words mean? On the one hand, the Lord calls for justice and righteousness instead of religious observances (5:21-24). On the other hand, the opposite of justice and righteousness is to cheat the poor (5:10-15), to corrupt the courts (5:10), and to deal unfairly in business, especially against the needy (8:4-6). Justice is a legal and a social term, concerning human behavior in society. To do justice, according to Amos, is to act with fairness, and to give all persons their legal rights. If Amos stresses that the rights of the poor and the needy are abused, it is because the Old Testament understands that the law is to protect the weak. The prophet addresses those who had the power both to do injustice and to establish justice. Wealth itself is not evil. But those who have become wealthy by treading on the poor corrupt justice.

Righteousness is a more explicitly religious term, referring to the quality of a life committed to a righteous God. The roots of just actions toward others lie in righteousness. Together the two terms stress the way persons live their lives, acting fairly toward others because of the quality of their faith.

When we call for justice, that call amounts to an accusation that justice is not being done. Should individual Christians, or the church, call for justice? If so, in what specific ways? If not, why not?

Amos 7:10-17—Prophets and the State

The conflict between Amos and Amaziah amounted to a confrontation between political and religious authority. As a representative of the king, the priest accused the prophet of conspiracy against the state. Given ancient Israel's understanding of the power of prophetic words to bring about what they said, Amaziah's accusation was true. Moreover, he had both the authority and the power to expel Amos. The prophet, however, appealed to a higher authority.

What parallels exist in our time to this ancient conflict? When moral decisions are made, when do religious values come into conflict with the laws or authority of a government? How do these present situations parallel the conflict between Amos and Amaziah? In what ways are they different?

*See, I will make you small among
the nations. . . (Obadiah 2).*

— 6 —

*God's People
Among the Nations*

Obadiah and Jonah

DIMENSION ONE:
WHAT DOES THE BIBLE SAY?

Answer these questions by reading Obadiah

1. Which nation does Obadiah's vision concern? (verse 1)

2. What does the Lord plan to do to Edom? (verse 2)

3. Why does the Lord announce disaster for Edom so that shame will cover them? (verse 10)

4. What should Edom not have done? (verse 12)

5. What will happen to all the nations on the day of the Lord? (verses 15-16)

6. What will the houses of Jacob, Joseph, and Esau be? (verse 18)

7. Who will go up on Mount Zion and govern the mountains of Esau? (verse 21)

Answer these questions by reading Jonah 1

8. Where does the Lord command Jonah to go, what is he to do, and why? (1:2)

9. Why does Jonah go to Joppa and board a ship to Tarshish? (1:3)

10. What do the sailors do when the storm threatens to break up the ship? (1:5)

11. Why are the sailors afraid when Jonah tells them who he is? (1:10)

12. What do the sailors do to Jonah? (1:12-16)

13. How long is Jonah inside the fish? (1:17)

Answer these questions by reading Jonah 2

14. What does Jonah say the Lord did for him? (2:5-6)

15. What does the fish do when the Lord speaks to it? (2:10)

Answer these questions by reading Jonah 3

16. What does Jonah do when God speaks to him again?
    (3:1-3)

17. What does Jonah proclaim as he goes through Nineveh?
    (3:4)

18. What does the king of Nineveh do when he hears the
    news? (3:6-8)

19. Why does the king of Nineveh send the proclamation? (3:9)

20. What does God do after seeing that the people of Nineveh have turned from their evil ways? (3:10)

Answer these questions by reading Jonah 4

21. How does Jonah respond to God's decision not to destroy Nineveh? (4:1)

22. What does Jonah do, and why? (4:5)

23. What is the Lord's final word to the angry prophet? (4:11)

DIMENSION TWO:
WHAT DOES THE BIBLE MEAN?

This lesson covers two very different books. Obadiah, the shortest book in the Old Testament, is a series of prophecies concerning God's reign. Its central theme is that the Lord will punish the enemies of Israel. In particular, God will punish their ancient adversary and neighbor, Edom.

The Book of Jonah is unique among the prophetic literature. It is not a collection of the addresses of a prophet. It is the study of a reluctant prophet who becomes bitter when God does not destroy Nineveh. Both books, then, address the same issue, the relationship of the people of God to foreign nations.

But their answers are radically different. The Book of Obadiah calls for revenge and the Book of Jonah calls for understanding and acceptance.

❏ *Obadiah.* The Book of Obadiah consists of only twenty-one verses. Nothing is known of the prophet except his name. *Obadiah* is possibly not a name but a title, meaning "worshiper of Yahweh" or "servant of Yahweh." The date and historical circumstances of the prophet and the book are far from certain. But on the basis of historical allusions, the book must be dated after the destruction of Jerusalem in 587 B.C. Obadiah perhaps could be dated as early as the Babylonian Exile or as late as the first half of the fifth century.

In terms of theme, type of literature, and possibly also authorship, the book has two major parts, verses 1-14 and 15b, and verses 15a, 16-21. The first part is a prophecy of destruction against Edom. The second part is an announcement concerning the coming day of the Lord. The second part concludes with the promise of the establishment of the kingdom of God. Like the Book of Joel, Obadiah bears the marks of liturgical use. It serves in the context of worship to reassure a troubled people that God will triumph in the end. The Edomites will be repaid for their participation in Israel's destruction.

❏ *Obadiah 1 4.* Following the superscription or title of the book, these verses comprise a prophecy of punishment against the nation of Edom. The prophecy sets the theme of the book—Edom, who had been proud and arrogant, will be brought low. Edom was one of the neighbors of Israel. The country was located on the southeast border of Judah. According to tradition, Edom descended from Esau, the brother of Jacob (Genesis 25:22-26).

❏ *Obadiah 5-10.* The punishment of Edom is described in greater detail. At first (verses 5-7) the speaker appears to describe events that have already taken place. It then becomes clear (verses 8-9) that he is announcing the future. In verse 10 the reason for punishment is given.

❏ *Obadiah 11-14, 15b.* Now the prophet details the reasons for the announcement of punishment against Edom. Their actions and words against Judah and Jerusalem are described.

All these offenses are seen to have taken place when Jerusalem was destroyed by the Babylonians in 586 B.C. Edom failed to come to the aid of Judah (verse 11). Rather, Edom gloated and rejoiced over his brother's misfortune (verse 12). They looted the city, and even aided the Babylonians by handing over survivors to them (verse 14). The conclusion, though vindictive, is a classical statement of justice: "As you have done, it will be done to you" (verse 15).

❏ *Obadiah 15a, 16.* The coming day of the Lord will encompass all nations. The people of Edom, in particular, will be like persons poisoned by what they drank on the holy mountain in Jerusalem.

❏ *Obadiah 17-21.* The counterpart to the punishment of Edom on the day of the Lord will be the escape and restoration of the people of the Lord. This victory will restore the kingdoms of Israel and Judah. Rulers (or deliverers or saviors) in Jerusalem will rule the Lord's kingdom, including Mount Esau in Edom.

❏ *Jonah.* Most prophetic books consist of a series of prophetic speeches. The Book of Jonah is unique. A narrative story about a prophet, it contains only one brief prophetic speech. (See Jonah 3:4.)

The book is a prophetic narrative in two senses, though. First, it is about a prophet and similar in many ways to other stories of prophets. Second, the story presents a message that is parallel to that of the most powerful prophetic voices in the Old Testament.

The book is Old Testament narrative at its best. It includes a carefully developed plot with subplots. The characters are subtly defined, and the descriptions of the settings are clearly drawn. The book has action, color, humor, and drama.

❏ *Jonah 1:1-3.* Jonah did not accept the call to go to Nineveh. Instead, Jonah booked passage on a boat headed in the opposite direction. Jonah's reaction is not unlike that of the resistance of others called by God. Moses (Exodus 3–4), Gideon (Judges 6), and Jeremiah (Jeremiah 1:4-10) were all reluctant to be called.

❏ *Jonah 1:4-16.* The second scene takes place on the boat bound for Tarshish. Its focus is upon the contrast between the prophet and the pagan sailors. When the storm comes, Jonah is asleep. The sailors are both working hard to save the ship and praying to their gods. When Jonah is found, the captain rebukes him for not praying. When the lots are cast, they reveal that the prophet is the cause of the problem. The sailors are awestruck to hear of "the LORD, the God of heaven, who made the sea and the land" (verse 9). Only reluctantly and with his permission do they throw Jonah overboard. When the sea settles down, they offer sacrifices and vows to God. They have become converts to a new faith.

❏ *Jonah 1:17–2:10.* Two verses of narrative (1:17 and 2:10) report on the "great fish" that swallowed up Jonah. This narrative is interrupted to report Jonah's prayer from the belly of the fish. Readers of the book often misinterpret the role of the fish and consequently the nature of the prayer. The prayer is a psalm of thanksgiving, not a petition for help. God sent the fish not as a threat but as a means to rescue Jonah from the sea.

❏ *Jonah 3:1-4.* This scene parallels the first one in the book. The Lord repeats the commission to Jonah to go to Nineveh. This time the prophet does as he is told. The message is a simple announcement of judgment upon the city. It does not give reasons for the judgment. Nor does it give alternatives or call to repent and be saved.

❏ *Jonah 3:5-10.* Like the pagan sailors who responded to Jonah's confession of faith, the king and citizens of Nineveh accept the prophet's message and decide to do something about it. Then the Lord responds to the sincere faith of the foreigners and "did not bring upon them the destruction he had threatened" (verse 10).

❏ *Jonah 4:1-11.* The final scene consists primarily of dialogue between God and Jonah. These verses focus on the attitude of the Israelite prophet toward God's grace for the foreigners. Jonah is angry at God. Jonah feels God made him look like a fool by announcing a judgment that did not come. He felt God was too kind. Jonah continues to sulk and complain. As God points out, Jonah is more concerned about a vine that shaded him than for Nineveh. God is concerned for all living creatures, even cattle.

GOD'S PEOPLE AMONG THE NATIONS

DIMENSION THREE:
WHAT DOES THE BIBLE MEAN TO ME?

Obadiah 20–21—The Elect and Outsiders

One Old Testament response to outsiders was to consider them enemies. Obadiah expected justice as retribution on those enemies. The emphasis is on the election of a particular group or people. Even when the reign of God over the world is expected, as in Obadiah 20–21, the foreigners are seen to have a subordinate place. In the light of the New Testament, the message of Jonah will appear more attractive to most Christians. The foreigners in the story of Jonah are presented in an altogether positive light. The narrow and vengeful attitude of the Lord's prophet is held up to ridicule. The author of Jonah criticizes the religious and national parochialism of many of his own people. Where in the church today would the author's criticisms also apply?

Jonah and the Mission of the Faithful

The Book of Jonah has long been considered one of the most powerful biblical passages that call the faithful to spread the word of their God to all peoples. Christian readers often have seen the book as a prelude to the commission of Jesus that concludes the Gospel of Matthew. (See Matthew 28:19-21.) But Jonah has no commands or instructions. Its message comes to the readers indirectly in a narrative. Still, the point is clear and the challenge to the faithful inescapable. God can and does use reluctant and even quarrelsome people to spread the word to the ends of the earth. Can you think of other examples?

*Hear this, you leaders of the house of Jacob, / you
rulers of the house of Israel, / who despise justice . . . (3:9).*

— 7 —
Judgment on Jerusalem
Micah 1–3

DIMENSION ONE:
WHAT DOES THE BIBLE SAY?

Answer these questions by reading Micah 1

1. When did the word of the Lord come to Micah? (1:1)

2. Who is called to hear? (1:2)

3. What will happen when God comes forth? (1:3-4)

4. Why are Jacob and Israel being punished? (1:5)

5. What will happen to Samaria? (1:6-7)

6. Why does God promise to weep and wail? (1:8-9)

7. What has come down from the Lord to the gate of Jerusa-lem? (1:12)

8. Why is Lachish called to harness the team to the chariot? (1:13)

Answer these questions by reading Micah 2

9. What do those who plan iniquity and plot evil do at morning's light? (2:1-2)

10. What will people say when they wail? (2:4)

11. What do "their" prophets say to Micah? (2:6)

12. What kind of prophet (or preacher) does Micah say the people want to have? (2:11)

13. What does the Lord promise to do to the remnant of Israel? (2:12)

14. To whom is this chapter addressed? (3:1)

15. How do the evil rulers treat God's people? (3:2-3)

16. Why will the Lord refuse to answer the leaders? (3:4)

17. Of what are the prophets accused? (3:5)

18. What will happen to the seers and the diviners? (3:7)

19. What does Micah claim about himself? (3:8)

20. What have the rulers done? (3:9-10)

21. How does Micah summarize his accusations against the leaders, the priests, and the prophets? (3:11)

DIMENSION TWO:
WHAT DOES THE BIBLE MEAN?

The Book of Micah is a collection of prophetic speeches. It contains both prophecies of judgment and prophecies of salvation. The book has two major sections, each with two parts. The first section is Micah 1–5. Chapters 1–3 consist almost entirely of prophecies of punishment. Chapters 4–5 contain prophecies of salvation. The second section, Micah 6–7, moves again from punishment (Micah 6:1–7:6) to salvation (Micah 7:7-20).

❏ *Micah 1–3.* These chapters are a series of prophecies of punishment. They are addressed to the capital cities of both the Northern and Southern Kingdoms. They include indictments of the leaders and main officials, including prophets. The message of these chapters is straightforward. The corruption and selfishness of their leaders will cause Samaria and Jerusalem to fall to their enemies.

❏ *Micah 1:1.* This single verse contains most of the information available to us concerning the prophet Micah. The superscription was not written by the prophet himself, but by a later editor of the book. Micah was a younger contemporary of Isaiah. He probably was not active for the full forty-six years of the reigns of the three kings listed here (741–687 B.C.). We date his work toward the end of the eighth century, before 701 B.C. Micah had a sense of divine justice. The outrage he felt because that justice had been perverted is similar to that of the other three prophets of the eighth century, Amos, Hosea, and Isaiah.

Micah is referred to elsewhere in the Old Testament (Jeremiah 26:18). He is mentioned in the context of Jeremiah's trial for preaching against the Temple in Jerusalem. Some of the princes and the people recall that, in the reign of Hezekiah, Micah of Moresheth prophesied that Zion and Jerusalem would be destroyed. Hezekiah did not put him to death.

Moresheth was a small town about twenty-five miles southwest of Jerusalem. As Micah's words indicate and the account in Jeremiah confirms, he was not content to stay at home. He went to the center of political and religious power to deliver his message.

Micah was the only eighth-century prophet who addressed his speeches to both the Northern and Southern Kingdoms, Samaria and Jerusalem. As in the other prophetic books, those words are specifically identified as divine revelation, "the word of the Lord."

❏ *Micah 1:2-7.* The announcement of punishment concerns Samaria, though (verses 6-8). Possibly this speech was given after the fall of Samaria to the Assyrian army in 721 B.C.

The speech begins with a call to start a trial. "Hear, O peoples . . . / listen, O earth . . ." (verse 2) is similar to the "Hear ye, hear ye" of some modern courtroom procedures. A special kind of trial is about to begin. The entire earth is called into court, and God will be a witness. Similar prophetic lawsuits are found elsewhere in the Old Testament (Hosea 4:1-6; Isaiah 1:2; Malachi 3:5). The Lord is a witness, but also is prosecutor and judge. After the call to court, the prophet describes the awesome appearance of the Lord (verses 3-4). The indictment is then introduced. The indictment gives the reason for the Lord's appearance to judge (verse 5). The speech concludes with the announcement of judgment upon Samaria. Samaria will be laid waste and its idols destroyed (verses 6-7).

❏ *Micah 1:8-16.* These verses are a lament or dirge sung over Jerusalem. The lines are in the poetic meter used for such songs. Verse 10 echoes expressions from the famous lament of David over Saul and Jonathan (2 Samuel 1:17-27, especially verse 20). What is the occasion for a funeral song over the capital city? The sin of Samaria has reached Jerusalem as well (verses 8-9). The people should mourn for the city because God announces that they will be conquered (verse 15) and the people will be exiled (verse 16).

❏ *Micah 2:1-5.* Micah directs his words against a particular group of people. He is speaking to those who are adding to their estates by means of force and oppression. The prophet announces the judgment of God upon the wealthy and powerful landowners (verses 3-5).

The wickedness that concerns the prophet is that powerful people covet and take the fields and houses of others. In ancient Israel a person's land and house were his "inheritance" (verse 2). That word goes back to the ancient biblical view of land ownership. The Israelites believed the land belonged to the Lord. It was handed over to a particular tribe and family in perpetuity. (See Joshua 13–19.) Land was inherited, not simply from one's ancestors, but from God. Taking another's inheritance violated the will of God.

Punishment is announced first in general terms. God is planning disaster against this people (verse 3). Then the punishment is spelled out as consistent with the crime (verses 4-5). The greedy want the property boundaries moved and land to change hands. That is just what will happen. Their fields will be divided among their captors.

❑ *Micah 2:6-11.* Here we suddenly find ourselves listening to an argument. The prophet is responding to his opponents. He begins by quoting their words (verses 6-7). They are not identified, but are probably the powerful landowners addressed in the previous verses. According to Micah, his hearers have urged him not to "prophesy about these things." They do not want to hear his announcements of disaster. They are convinced that God would not do such things to them. In the remaining verses (8-11), the prophet presents his side of the argument. He points out just how unjust the people are. They act with violence against the peaceful. They dispossess women and children. Their deeds bring "uncleanness." This in turn brings destruction (verse 10). The kind of preacher these people want is one who utters lies and preaches of wine and strong drink (verse 11).

❑ *Micah 2:12-13.* These verses are in sharp contrast to the previous verses. This speech is an announcement of salvation of the "remnant of Israel" (verse 12). The first of two images is that of the scattered people gathered like a peaceful flock of sheep. The second image is that of a procession including the king with God at the head.

❑ *Micah 3:1-4.* This speech is the first of a series against the leaders of Israel. Here Micah indicts the political authorities. They, above all, are responsible for justice. They should know how to love the good and hate the evil. Instead they oppress the people (verse 2). Their punishment is that in the time of trouble they will cry, but God will not answer them (verse 4).

❑ *Micah 3:5-8.* Next Micah conveys the word of God concerning other prophets. They are identified and condemned as ones who cry "peace" when fed. but they call for war against those who will not feed them (verse 5). As we have already seen (Micah 2:11), they are the kind of prophets the people want. The punishment fits the crime. There will be no vision, divination, or light for such prophets. They will be disgraced (verses 6-7). Micah, on the other hand, states in the strongest possible terms that he is filled with power. He has the Spirit of the Lord.

❑ *Micah 3:9-12.* Another prophecy of punishment summarizes the indictment of the leaders of the people and the results that will follow. The prophet addresses the "leaders" and "rulers," but also includes the priests and the prophets. All these leaders "despise justice," deal corruptly, and have false confidence that God is on their side (verses 9-11). But, because of them, Zion, the Temple mountain, and Jerusalem, the Holy City, will become deserted ruins.

DIMENSION THREE:
WHAT DOES THE BIBLE MEAN TO ME?

True and False Prophets

More than once Micah addresses the question of true and false prophecy. In a debate with his audience (Micah 2:6-11), the prophet responds to objections that he is preaching the wrong thing. By appealing to their understanding of God as a gracious God and to their own good works, the people in effect accuse Micah of being a false prophet. They claim he does not preach the true word of God. In the process of cataloging the sins of Israel's leaders, Micah indicts the prophets who lead the people astray. These prophets announce peace when they have something to eat, but call for war against those who do not feed them (Micah 3:5-7). He accuses such people of being false prophets.

The problem was not new in the time of Micah. It persisted in ancient Israel. A great many individuals arose to speak to the people in the name of the Lord. But often different prophets delivered contradictory messages in the name of the same god. One famous controversy took place in the time of Jeremiah. A prophet named Hananiah appeared with a message of good news. Jeremiah was preaching words of judgment (Jeremiah 27–28). How was one to know who was the true prophet? Ancient Israel had several tests in different periods— the true prophet is the one who announces judgment, the true prophet is the one whose words come true, and no true prophet leads the people to worship false gods.

The problem continues today as we hear various claims about the future that God intends for the world. As if we understand a prophet to be one who speaks the word of God, the truth, then the problem is a daily one for us. Who speaks the truth for God? How do we know? How can the study of the Bible, and especially of the Old Testament prophets, help us resolve such questions? Micah had no doubt at all that he was called by God, filled with power, the Spirit of the Lord, and with justice and might (Micah 3:8).

What does the LORD require of you? / To act justly and to love mercy / and to walk humbly with your God (6:8).

8

God's Peaceful Reign
Micah 4–7

DIMENSION ONE:
WHAT DOES THE BIBLE SAY?

Answer these questions by reading Micah 4

1. What will be established as chief among the mountains and raised above the hills? (4:1)

2. Why will the people come to the mountain? (4:1)

3. What will the people do with their swords and their spears? (4:3)

4. What will God do with the lame and with the exiles? (4:6-7)

5. Where will the people of Jerusalem be rescued and redeemed? (4:10)

6. What is the Daughter of Zion to do with the wealth of many peoples? (4:13)

Answer these questions by reading Micah 5

7. Who is to come forth from Bethlehem Ephrathah? (5:2)

8. What will the ruler do? (5:4)

9. What are the "seven shepherds" and "eight leaders of men" to do? (5:5-6)

10. What is the remnant of Jacob to be like among the nations? (5:8)

11. What will the Lord destroy in that day? (5:10-13)

Answer these questions by reading Micah 6

12. What does God call to hear the accusation against the people? (6:2)

13. What has God done for the people? (6:4-5)

14. What does God require? (6:8)

15. What does God ask about the ill-gotten treasures, the short ephah (a dry measure), and the man with dishonest scales and a bag of false weights? (6:10-11)

16. Why has the Lord begun to destroy the people? (6:13)

17. Whose statutes and practices have the people kept? (6:16)

Answer these questions by reading Micah 7

18. Who has been swept from the land? (7:2)

19. What do the ruler, the judge, and the powerful do? (7:3)

20. How do children treat their parents? (7:6)

21. What does the prophet say he will do? (7:7)

22. What will God do for the prophet? (7:9)

23. What will happen to the enemy? (7:10)

24. What will the Lord do for the people as in the days when they came out of Egypt? (7:15)

25. To whom will the nations turn? (7:17)

DIMENSION TWO:
WHAT DOES THE BIBLE MEAN?

Chapters 4–7 include a collection of promises, a series of prophecies of punishment, and a collection of announcements of salvation. The most persistent theme is God's coming peaceful reign.

❑ *Micah 4:1-4.* This passage is almost identical to Isaiah 2:2-4. It is one of the most powerful and compelling promises in the Bible. The prophet announces that one day God will begin a reign of eternal peace. God will establish and maintain justice. People will turn instruments of war into agricultural implements. No wars will be waged, and no military training will be needed. Fear will be banished. All peoples will be at peace with one another.

No date is set for the establishment of the reign of peace. The expression *in the last days* (verse 1) refers simply to some time in the future. The era of peace will come within history and not beyond time. Moreover, God's reign is to come on the earth, with Jerusalem as the center.

❑ *Micah 4:6-8.* These words are an announcement of salvation to the city of Jerusalem.

❑ *Micah 4:9-10.* What begins as a lament becomes in these verses an announcement of salvation. Zion, personified as a woman in labor, cries and groans. When she goes to Babylon, the Lord will rescue her and redeem her from her enemies.

❑ *Micah 4:11-13.* These words contain good news for Zion. But they are actually an announcement of judgment upon the enemies of Israel. Singled out in particular are those who call for Zion to be profaned and ridiculed. Such people do not understand what the Lord has in mind. The Lord calls upon Zion to thresh them and devote their gain and wealth to God.

❑ *Micah 5:1-6.* Like the previous section, this speech moves from a description of the present trouble to an announcement of salvation. The present trouble is a siege of Jerusalem and the abuse of the king of Israel (verse 1). Salvation will come first when a new ruler comes out of Bethlehem. This ruler will "shepherd his flock in the strength of the LORD" and see to it that they dwell secure (verses 2-4). Then peace will come when "seven shepherds, even eight leaders of men" are raised up to deliver Israel from the Assyrian threat (verses 5-6). The vision of Israel's salvation focuses upon a new king in the line of David. David came from Bethlehem. The king is the anointed one of God, the messiah. The prophet must have expected the righteous king to come soon enough for deliverance from the Assyrian threat.

❑ *Micah 5:7-9.* These words of good news concern the "remnant of Jacob." The remnant is scattered among the peoples of the world. Though they are few, and they are separated from their homeland, their strength comes from God. For this reason, they shall survive and triumph over their enemies. The final verse is a blessing that the people have power over their enemies. This blessing might have been used in worship.

❑ *Micah 6:1-5.* As in Micah 1:2, God calls the people into court. God will be both attorney for the prosecution and judge. Verses 1-2 initiate the hearing. They indicate that God has an "accusation" or legal complaint with Israel. In the rest of the speech (verses 3-5), God builds a defense against an accusation by the people.

GOD'S PEACEFUL REIGN

❑ *Micah 6:6-8.* The people respond to the Lord's charges by asking what God requires of them. With sincerity, they go through a list of possibilities, even raising the questions of human sacrifice (verse 7). The answer, while it does not directly reject such possibilities, turns the matter around. They have asked "with what shall I come before the LORD?" The prophetic answer reminds them that God already has what is good. The Lord expects three things. These things all have to do with the quality of human life in society. The people should act justly, love mercy, and walk humbly with God. These words constitute a prophetic definition of the life of faith and religion. They were nothing new to the hearers ("he has showed you . . ."). The call for justice and kindness is a familiar cry throughout the Old Testament. "To walk humbly with your God" is a call to follow the will of God. This advice is not an addition to the others, but a summary of them. Moreover, the definition of what is good applies to all persons, men and women.

❑ *Micah 6:9-16.* The prophet presents the words of the Lord accusing the people of their sins (verses 9-12, 16a) and announcing punishment because of those actions (verses 13-15, 16b). "The city" is Jerusalem. The wickedness of the people includes cheating in business, violence, lies, and obeying the laws of the northern kings Omri and Ahab. Omri and Ahab led the people away from the pure worship of God. The punishment, which has already begun, will include a series of disasters. Finally, the Lord will destroy the city and see that its inhabitants are ridiculed.

❑ *Micah 7:1-7.* A song describes the evil of the society. It hardly seems safe to go into the streets. Even among friends and family there is decay in the moral order. The singer concludes on the positive note of confidence in the Lord, in spite of the trouble all around.

❑ *Micah 7:8-20.* This section concludes the book. In verses 8-10 an individual, possibly personified Jerusalem, expresses confidence that God will deliver her from her enemy. Verses 11-13 are an announcement of salvation. The walls of Jerusalem will be rebuilt. Its inhabitants who are now scattered will return. But the other peoples will suffer for their evil deeds. Verse 14

66   THE MINOR PROPHETS

is a prayer that God cares for the people as in the ancient days. In verses 15-17, that prayer is answered when God promises to do "wonders." The nations will be afraid and turn to God. The final verses (18-20) are a hymn of praise for the incomparable God. God is incomparable by being willing to pardon sin. God is the one who delights "to show mercy."

DIMENSION THREE: WHAT DOES THE BIBLE MEAN TO ME?

Micah 6:6-8—True Religion

Micah 6:8 poses the question, "What does the LORD require of you?" It also gives the answer in three concise phrases that summarize the prophetic understanding of true religion: "act justly, love mercy, walk humbly with your God." The first two phrases define human activity in response to the nature of God. God is just; do justice. God abounds in steadfast love; so should you. The third phrase emphasizes the submission of the human will to the Divine. Are *justice* and *mercy* the same? In the Old Testament they are not sharply distinguished from each other, but each helps to define the other.

The context of Micah 6:8 focuses for us a particular question concerning true religion and the life of faith. The verse is preceded by a series of questions concerning worship. These questions list the possible sacrifices and offerings that the religious person might bring to God. In our time, the question would focus upon church worship and other acts of prayer and devotion. Does the prophet mean to suggest that God requires justice, mercy, and humility instead of acts of public and private worship? It seems unlikely that Micah envisions a life of faith without worship. What is the relationship between piety and behavior in society?

Micah 4:1-4—The Power of Promise

These chapters contain numerous announcements of the salvation that God has in store for Israel, and even for the entire world. None of these statements is more powerful and compelling than the lines in Micah 4:1-4. These verses are a promise of perfect and eternal peace in the world. In the name of the God who created the heavens and the earth, the prophet announces that a time will come when war shall cease.

Do such promises have any meaning or power in a world that constantly faces the threat and the reality of military conflict? Our century has hardly known a day when people were not at war somewhere on the globe. Even little children fear the outbreak of a war that could certainly spell the end of war, as well as the end of civilization. Is the promise of Micah 4:1-4 naive and unrealistic in our time?

But think about the power of promises, and of visions. Even human promises sometimes have the power to change the future. When a man and a woman promise to be faithful "until death do us part," lives are changed. Even those who do not stay married are led forward by promises they have made to one another. Or think of living in a world in which the promise, the hope, the vision of peace was not heard. Is it true that without a vision the people perish? According to Micah 4:1-4, it is God's wish that all peoples of the earth live together in peace. How can Christians be spokespersons of that hope, that promise?

The LORD is a jealous and avenging God; / the LORD
takes vengeance and is filled with wrath . . . (Nahum 1:2).

9

God's Justice
and Vengeance
Nahum and Habakkuk

DIMENSION ONE:
WHAT DOES THE BIBLE SAY?

Answer these questions by reading Nahum 1

1. What does the oracle concern, and how is the Book of
   Nahum described? (1:1)

2. What is the Lord's way? (1:3)

3. What happens when the Lord appears? (1:5)

4. What is the Lord to "those who trust in him"? (1:7)

5. What does God promise to cut off from the temple of their gods? (1:14)

Answer these questions by reading Nahum 2

6. What are people told to do? (2:1)

7. How are the chariots described? (2:4)

8. What is Nineveh like? (2:8)

Answer these questions by reading Nahum 3

9. How does the prophet describe "the city of blood"? (3:1-3)

10. What will those who look at Nineveh say? (3:7)

11. What nations and peoples were Nineveh's strength and allies? (3:9)

12. What has happened to Nineveh's infants and nobles? (3:10)

13. Why do those who hear the news of the king of Assyria clap their hands? (3:19)

Answer these questions by reading Habakkuk 1

14. What is the prophet's initial complaint to the Lord? (1:2-4)

15. What nation is God raising up, and what do they do? (1:6)

16. What is the god of the Babylonians, the guilty men who "sweep past like the wind"? (1:11)

17. What does Habakkuk ask God? (1:13)

Answer these questions by reading Habakkuk 2

18. What does God command the prophet concerning the vision? (2:2)

19. What does God say about the one whose desires are not upright and the one who is righteous? (2:4)

20. What is to happen to the one who makes his neighbors drink to the point of drunkenness? (2:15-17)

21. What does a workman do when he carves an idol? (2:18-19)

Answer these questions by reading Habakkuk 3

22. What does Habakkuk ask of God? (3:2)

23. What did God do when coming out to deliver the people? (3:13-15)

24. What does the prophet say he will wait patiently for? (3:16)

25. What does the prophet say he will do though the harvest and herds fail? (3:17-18)

DIMENSION TWO:
WHAT DOES THE BIBLE MEAN?

Nahum and Habakkuk are similar in some respects. In other respects they are quite distinct. Both prophets focus upon God's punishment of the enemies of Judah and the consequent good news for the people of God. These books are quite different from the earlier prophetic books such as Amos,

Hosea, and Micah. The earlier books prophesy judgment upon the people of Israel for their sins. Both books include hymns and prayers that were probably used on liturgical occasions. The most obvious marks of this use are the hymns in Nahum 1 and Habakkuk 3.

The Book of Nahum celebrates the downfall of the Assyrian Empire and the destruction of Nineveh in 612 B.C. Habakkuk has two major parts. Chapters 1 and 2 are a dialogue between the prophet and God. Habakkuk asks why the Lord allows the people to suffer at the hands of their enemies. Chapter 3 is a hymn celebrating God's victory over the enemies of Judah.

❑ *Nahum 1:1.* Here are two titles to the book. The first identifies the book in terms of its content, the second in terms of its author. The term *oracle* could also be translated "burden." It often is used as the heading for prophecies of judgment against the enemies of Israel for Judah. Virtually the entire book concerns the fall of Nineveh.

❑ *Nahum 1:2-11.* The Book of Nahum begins with a hymn to the terrible power of God. The hymn speaks of God's vengeance on Israel's enemies and God's mercy for those who have faith. The emphasis falls upon God's vengeance. Verses 2-3a state the general doctrine of wrath for adversaries of God. The Lord who is "slow to anger" will still punish the guilty. Verses 3b-5 describe God's appearance in terms of whirlwind and storm. With rhetorical questions and affirmations of faith, verses 6-11 emphasize that none can endure the anger of God. But God is also a "refuge in times of trouble" (verse 7).

❑ *Nahum 1:12–2:2.* The persons who are addressed and referred to in this passage are not clear. The enemy is probably Nineveh, the major city of the Assyrian Empire. These verses announce that Judah and Jerusalem are to be freed from the threat of the Assyrians.

In 1:12-13 God speaks directly to the people of Judah ("you"). God promises that though the Assyrians ("they") are strong and numerous, God will break Nineveh's ("their") yoke. In verse 14 the Lord addresses Nineveh, or perhaps the king of Nineveh, with an announcement that its idols will be destroyed. Nineveh is headed for the grave. Verse 15 is an unqualified announcement of salvation to Judah, as is Nahum 2:2. Nahum 2:1 seems to address a warning to Nineveh.

❏ *Nahum 2:3-12.* The prophet describes the battle that ends with Nineveh's capture and destruction. Nineveh, who had been like a proud lion that took prey home to its cubs, has itself become the prey of others.

❏ *Nahum 2:13–3:7.* The poem begins and ends with direct addresses to Nineveh. God pronounces destruction upon the city. In the rest of the speech (3:1-4), the prophet returns to the scene of the final battle in the city. Chaos and death are everywhere. Two themes dominate the poem. First, God will bring death and destruction upon the once powerful city "who enslaved nations by her prostitution" (3:4). Second, God will shame and embarrass the once proud Nineveh. Her nakedness will be exposed so that none will mourn or comfort her.

❏ *Nahum 3:8-19.* The book concludes with a song in which the prophet heaps ridicule upon Nineveh. Nineveh is no better than Thebes. Thebes was well protected and had strong allies, but still was carried away (verses 8-10). Nineveh will seek refuge, but the fortresses and walls will be weak, the soldiers ineffective, and the gates open to the enemy (verses 11-13). No matter how hard the people work to prepare for the siege they will be taken by fire and sword (verses 14-15). Nineveh's merchants, princes, and scribes may multiply, but they shall disappear. A final taunt is addressed to the king of Assyria himself (verses 18-19). His military leaders are asleep, his people scattered without direction, and his wounds are fatal. Moreover, all who hear the news will celebrate, for everyone has suffered at his hand.

❏ *Habakkuk 1:1.* Like Nahum, the Book of Habakkuk is identified as an oracle, a divine revelation to the prophet. The title identifies Habakkuk only as "the prophet," and gives no clues about his date or circumstances.

❏ *Habakkuk 1:1–2:5.* The first section of the book records a dialogue between the prophet and God. The dialogue concerns a single issue, stated at the outset—why do the wicked oppress the righteous so that justice is perverted? First the prophet complains. He asks how long he has to cry to God about the trouble and violence around him (verses 2-4). Then

God responds (verses 5-11). God is doing a wondrous thing in the prophet's own time, which will bring justice. The Chaldeans, the Babylonians, have been called up by God to act against the wicked. The prophet responds with a second complaint addressed to God (verses 12-17). This complaint is quite similar to the first one. Habakkuk wants to know why God is silent when the wicked swallow up the righteous (verse 13). The second complaint gets no immediate response. The prophet says he will take his stand to wait and watch, to see what God has to say (2:1). Then he reports (2:2-4) that an answer came, commanding him to write the vision so that it could be seen even by one who runs by. The people must wait patiently for the vision. When it finally comes, it will be a word of assurance that the righteous shall live by faith.

❑ *Habakkuk 2:5-20.* This section of the book is a series of woes indicting those who do wrong. The first woe (verses 6-8) concerns one who takes what does not belong to him, who plunders the nations. That one will in turn be plundered by "the peoples who are left." The second woe (verses 9-11) is against the one who "builds his realm by unjust gain." That one has forfeited his life. The third woe (verses 12-14) criticizes the one who builds a town with blood and is not consistent with God's purpose. This woe concludes with a promise that one day the earth will be filled with the knowledge of the glory of God. The fourth woe uses the image of a drinking context. It criticizes the one who "gives drink to his neighbors, pouring it from the wineskin till they are drunk" and humiliates them. That one will himself receive the wrath of God, and will be humiliated. The fifth woe (verses 18-20) addresses those who make and worship idols and images. This woe ridicules the idea. It concludes with the solemn statement that God is in the holy temple. The entire earth should be reverent before God.

❑ *Habakkuk 3:1-19.* The chapter has its own heading and conclusion, including instructions for its use in worship. The poem is identified as a "prayer of Habakkuk the prophet." The liturgical instructions (*Selah*) are identical to those found with many of the psalms. Thus we are again reminded that prophets could have roles in the priestly services of the Temple.

The body of the prayer (verses 3-15) is in fact a hymn, a song of praise. The remainder of the chapter forms the framework of God's work as of old. In verses 16-19 the prophet affirms that come what may he will wait in confidence for the Lord and rejoice.

DIMENSION THREE:
WHAT DOES THE BIBLE MEAN TO ME?

These two books contain a great many significant and memorable lines, including Habakkuk's words that Paul used to express the understanding that the righteous shall live by faith. They also contain hymns in praise of God's justice and might and well-known sentences such as, "The LORD is in his holy temple, / let all the earth be silent before him" (Habakkuk 2:20). However, the most persistent theme of both books, the vengeance of God on the enemies of Israel, is very difficult for most modern Christian readers.

The Vengeance of the Lord

The words of these books, which after all are part of our sacred Scriptures, are a challenge to our understanding. Prayers that the enemies be destroyed, and celebrations of the fact that "infants were dashed to pieces" (Nahum 3:10), jar the consciousness. Our beliefs have been shaped by the commandment to "love your enemies, do good to those who hate you, bless those who curse you, pray for those who mistreat you" (Luke 6:27-28; see also Matthew 5:44). So as we consider the meaning of these books for us we must acknowledge that they present a problem.

If we think of their meaning, then our first step is to hear Nahum and Habakkuk on their own terms. We should not try to make them say what we might prefer to hear. We will remember the historical context in which these voices arose. They come from a time when Israel and Judah had suffered from the Assyrian armies. These armies had destroyed the Northern Kingdom, and put the Southern Kingdom under its thumb. In the ancient world, *Assyria* was a word that struck terror in the hearts of those who lived in the small states in Syria and Palestine. Consequently, these books may be valuable to us by helping us see world events from the perspective of the victims of military oppression. We need not agree in order to understand the anger, hatred, and the cry for vengeance.

But finally we need to assess the validity of the point of view expressed in these books in the light of broader considerations. What is their message in the light of an understanding of the Bible as a whole, and especially in the light of the Gospel?

Seek the LORD, all you humble of the land . . . /
perhaps you will be sheltered / on the day of the LORD's anger
(Zephaniah 2:3).

— 10 —
The Reign of God
Zephaniah and Haggai

DIMENSION ONE:
WHAT DOES THE BIBLE SAY?

Answer these questions by reading Zephaniah 1

1. When did the word of the Lord come to Zephaniah? (1:1)

2. What does God say will be swept away? (1:1-2)

3. Who does God promise to punish on the day of the Lord's sacrifice? (1:8-9)

4. Who does the Lord promise to punish when searching out Jerusalem with lamps? (1:12)

5. What kind of day is the day of the Lord? (1:15-16)

THE MINOR PROPHETS

Answer these questions by reading Zephaniah 2

6. What is the shameful nation called to do? (2:1)

7. What are the humble of the land told to do? (2:3)

8. What threat does the "woe" cry introduce? (2:5)

9. Why are Moab and the Ammonites being punished? (2:8-9)

10. What does the prophet say will happen when God's hand is stretched out against the north? (2:13)

Answer these questions by reading Zephaniah 3

11. How does the oppressing city that is rebellious and defiled behave? (3:1-2)

12. What are the officials, rulers, prophets, and priests of the oppressing city like? (3:3-4)

13. Which people does God promise to remove? (3:11)

14. Why are the daughters of Zion and Israel rejoicing? (3:14-15)

Answer these questions by reading Haggai 1

15. When did the word of the Lord come to Haggai the prophet, and to whom was that word addressed? (1:1)

16. What do the people say concerning the Lord's house? (1:2)

17. What does God say through the prophet about the way the people have fared? (1:6)

18. Why have the people expected much and it turned out to be little? (1:9)

19. What did Zerubbabel, Joshua, and the people do? (1:12)

20. What happened on the twenty-fourth day of the sixth month? (1:14-15)

Answer these questions by reading Haggai 2

21. What does the Lord promise to do concerning the present house? (2:9)

22. What is the first question God instructs Haggai to ask the priests? (2:11-12)

23. What is Haggai's second question to the priests? (2:13)

24. What does the Lord promise to do to Zerubbabel, and why? (2:23)

DIMENSION TWO:
WHAT DOES THE BIBLE MEAN?

Zephaniah was active in the seventh century B.C., not long before 621 B.C.. The book has four parts. The first unit (1:2–2:3) announces judgment against Judah and Jerusalem. It includes the threat of the terrible day of the Lord. The second unit (2:4-15) is a series of woes against certain foreign nations. In the third section (3:1-13), the prophet returns to announcements of punishment against Jerusalem. The punishment will purify God's people and leave a remnant of those who seek the Lord. The final unit of the book (3:14-20) contains announcements of salvation to Jerusalem and expressions of celebration that such salvation has come.

The prophet Haggai was active about a century later than Zephaniah. All the oracles are dated quite precisely in the year 520 B.C. The book contains four oracles and one report of the response to an oracle. In the first oracle (1:1-11), the prophet instructs the people to rebuild the Temple. Next is the report (1:12-15) that the people began to do so. The second oracle (2:1-9) promises that the glory of the new Temple will surpass that of the former one. The people will prosper. In the third oracle (2:10-19), the prophet explains that while ritual uncleanness is contagious, holiness is not. The fourth and final oracle (2:20-23) announces that God has chosen Zerubbabel and will make him "like my signet ring."

❑ *Zephaniah 1:1.* This superscription is unusual. The prophet's ancestry is traced back four generations. If the Hezekiah mentioned is the king by that name, it would explain the long genealogy. It would also explain why Zephaniah spoke to Jerusalem and its ruling circles. Zephaniah was active in the time of King Josiah of Judah (640–609). Josiah led his people in a religious reformation and the renewal of the covenant with the Lord. Many concerns of that reformation are shared by the prophet.

❑ *Zephaniah 1:2–2:3.* The theme of this passage is the coming judgment. The judgment will take the form of the day of the Lord. The passage consists of several parts that originally may have been presented orally on different occasions. In most of the verses, God speaks directly. Now and then we hear the prophet speak to introduce the divine message. In 1:2-6 God threatens to destroy all life from the face of the earth. God will judge Judah and Jerusalem because the people worship false gods and idols. In 1:7-13 the prophet announces the day of the Lord as a time of judgment against the people of Jerusalem. Their leaders (verse 8) and those who say the Lord will do neither good nor ill (verse 12) will especially be judged. It will be a time of suffering and mourning. In 1:14-18 the day of the Lord is further described as a horrible time for the entire earth. Finally, the prophet himself speaks (2:1-3) to encourage all the "humble of the land" to call an assembly. They should seek God and seek righteousness and humility in order that they may be spared from the wrath of God on that day.

❑ *Zephaniah 2:4-15.* These verses contain a series of prophecies against foreign nations. The prophecies take up the enemies in a geographical order. First (2:4-7) the Philistines to the west of Judah are addressed. God will destroy the inhabitants of the Philistine territory along the coast. Second, Moab and Ammon to the east are condemned (2:8-11). Because of their pride the people of Judah shall plunder them and possess their land. Third is a brief announcement of judgment against Ethiopia to the south. Fourth, Assyria to the north and its chief city Nineveh are condemned to become a desolation (2:12-15).

❑ *Zephaniah 3:1-13.* Now the attention of the prophet is directed to Jerusalem. This announcement is quite different from those against the foreign powers. In the first place, the sins of the people are spelled out in greater detail. The city is accused of listening to no one and of not trusting in God (3:1-2). The officials, rulers, prophets, and priests are corrupt (3:3-4). God has destroyed the nations in order to warn Jerusalem, but in vain (3:6-7). Now God will act in judgment, but it will be a purging punishment. The speech of the peoples will be changed into a pure speech so that they call on the name of God (3:8-10). Finally, God will destroy those who are haughty, leaving those who are humble and lowly and who seek refuge in the name of the Lord (3:11-13).

❑ *Zephaniah 3:14-20.* The final passage of the book is a combination of shouts of celebration and announcements of salvation to Jerusalem. God promises to be in the midst of the city, to restore the fortunes of the people, to change shame into praise, and to bring the people home.

❑ *Haggai 1:1-11.* The first oracle of Haggai, like those that follow, is dated (verse 1) precisely. The second year of Darius would have been 520 B.C. The sixth month would have been mid-August through mid-September. The Persian king Darius ruled for almost four decades (522–185 B.C.) over an empire that included most of the ancient Near East. Judah was a province of that empire. Judah had its own governor and a wide measure of religious freedom. Cyrus, who established the Persian Empire, had captured the city of Babylon and allowed the exiles to begin returning home in 538 B.C.

The prophet addresses his message from God to the two leaders of the community, Zerubbabel, the governor appointed by the Persians, and Joshua, the high priest. But Haggai directs the contents of the message to the people as a whole. The point of the message is that God wants the people to begin rebuilding the Temple in Jerusalem. Because the Temple still lies in ruins, the heavens have refused to give moisture, the earth has withheld its produce, and God has brought a drought.

❑ *Haggai 1:12-15.* The first oracle is immediately followed by the report of the response of Zerubbabel, Joshua, and the people. They obeyed the instructions of Haggai because they were the word of God. In fact, it is emphasized that God stirred up the spirit of the leaders and the people. They began to work on the Temple within a month of Haggai's message.

❑ *Haggai 2:1-9.* Less than a month after the work began, during the Feast of Tabernacles, Haggai delivered a second oracle. This oracle is a word of assurance and encouragement, in view of a particular problem. Those who remember the former Temple, the structure built by Solomon, will consider the present building "like nothing" (verse 3). Moreover, the former Temple probably had become even greater in memory and tradition than it was in reality. The word of God, however, is that God is with them in accordance with the promise at the time of the Exodus. In the future God will "shake all nations" (verse 7) so that their treasures will come to the Temple. Its splendor will then exceed that of its predecessor. The prophet thus reassures the people on the basis of both the past and the promised future.

❑ *Haggai 2:10-19.* Three months to the day after the building began, Haggai presented both this oracle and the one that follows in 2:20-23. Here, upon instructions from God, Haggai asks the priests a technical question concerning holiness and ritual impurity. If something holy touches something ordinary, the ordinary does not become sacred. But on the other hand, if something unclean touches something holy, the holy becomes unclean. Haggai then draws a conclusion concerning the offerings (verse 14) that the people have brought up to the present time. For some unspecified reason they are judged to be unclean. Perhaps their impurity relates to the failure to build the Temple. Finally, Haggai promises that God will now begin to bless the people.

❑ *Haggai 2:20-23.* Haggai's final oracle is a promise of salvation addressed to Zerubbabel, the governor of Judah. The prophet announces the inauguration of God's kingdom. At that time the kingdoms of the world will be overthrown, and Zerubbabel, the chosen one, will reign. Haggai evokes the image of Zerubbabel as fulfilling the promise that one of the sons of David would always sit on the throne in Jerusalem (see 2 Samuel 7).

DIMENSION THREE:
WHAT DOES THE BIBLE MEAN TO ME?

The Reign of God and Human Responsibility

Both Zephaniah and Haggai base everything they say on the belief that God is about to act in their time. Zephaniah announced the day of the Lord as an occasion when God's enemies, both foreign and domestic, will be overthrown. The enemies are not only among the pagan nations, but within Israel. A righteous and devout remnant of the faithful will be left. Haggai announces that once the people rebuilt the Temple they would enjoy the blessings God wished to give them, and a new king in the line of David would reign. This king would come in history, in Jerusalem. Both prophets believed that God's kingdom was about to come to earth.

Human beings could not bring in such a Kingdom. Only God's intervention could bring these things about. However, each prophet considered certain human actions as essential. Zephaniah identifies idolatry and the worship of gods that are not God as contrary to the will of the Lord. Those who do not believe that God will act will have no place in the coming Kingdom. He says that God's new kingdom will be populated by those who seek humility. That vision is not unlike the Beatitudes. In those, Jesus says the poor in spirit shall have the kingdom of heaven, the meek shall inherit the earth, and the poor in heart shall see God (Matthew 5:3-8). Moreover, Zephaniah links such an attitude of humility and reverence directly to seeking righteousness (Zephaniah 2:3).

According to Haggai, God's gracious intentions toward the people cannot be realized until they begin to rebuild the Temple and become scrupulous about sacred things. We could easily say such a call is selfish and materialistic. Should we only build a temple or a church in order to become more prosperous? Haggai contains an element of such an attitude. But the central note is one of criticism. The people have become so preoccupied with their own economic well-being that they have neglected what is central. They have neglected their faith and worship. Certainly in the kingdom of God there are times and places that are particularly sacred, when homage is paid to the ruler of that Kingdom. How do the words of Jesus help us understand the meaning of this Old Testament text for our lives: "But seek first his kingdom and his righteousness, and all these things will be given to you as well" (Matthew 6:33; see also Luke 12:31)?

The city streets will be filled with boys and girls playing there (8:5).

11
Visions of Restoration
Zechariah 1–8

DIMENSION ONE:
WHAT DOES THE BIBLE SAY?

Answer these questions by reading Zechariah 1

1. How is Zechariah identified? (1:1)

2. What does God tell Zechariah to say to the people? (1:3)

3. What does Zechariah say he saw in the night? (1:8)

4. How did God answer the angel? (1:12-13)

5. What are the four horns? (1:18)

Answer these questions by reading Zechariah 2

6. What is the man with the measuring line in his hand going to do? (2:2)

7. What should those who are spread abroad as the four winds of heaven do? (2:6-7)

Answer these questions by reading Zechariah 3

8. Who is in Zechariah's vision? (3:1)

9. What does the angel say about the filthy clothes Joshua is wearing? (3:4)

10. What does the angel of the Lord promise Joshua if he walks in God's way? (3:7)

11. What will happen when God engraves an inscription on the stone set up before Joshua? (3:9-10)

Answer these questions by reading Zechariah 4

12. To whom is the message concerning the lampstand, the bowl, and the olive trees addressed? (4:6)

13. What is the word of the Lord concerning Zerubbabel? (4:8-9)

14. How does the angel answer Zechariah's questions concerning the meaning of the two olive trees and the two branches of the olive tree? (4:11-14)

Answer these questions by reading Zechariah 5

15. What does Zechariah see when he looks again? (5:1-2)

16. How is the meaning of the flying scroll explained to the prophet? (5:3-4)

17. What does the angel show Zechariah? (5:5-6)

18. What happened to the basket? (5:9-11)

Answer these questions by reading Zechariah 6

19. How many chariots does Zechariah see, and what kind of mountains did they come out of? (6:1)

20. Where are the four chariots going? (6:5)

21. What does God tell Zechariah to do with the silver and gold? (6:9-11)

Answer these questions by reading Zechariah 7

22. What is asked of the priests and the prophets? (7:2-3)

23. What is the word of God that came to Zechariah? (7:8-10)

24. Why would the Lord not hear when the people called? (7:13-14)

Answer these questions by reading Zechariah 8

25. What does God promise to do for Zion and Jerusalem? (8:3)

26. What are the people to do? (8:15-17)

27. In the days to come, what will ten men from all languages and nations do? (8:23)

DIMENSION TWO:
WHAT DOES THE BIBLE MEAN?

The first eight chapters of Zechariah contain the words of a prophet who was a contemporary of Haggai. Zechariah 1–8 contains three unequal parts. The first of these (1:1-6) is an introduction to the book. The introduction is in the form of the prophet's call to the people to repent and return to the Lord. The second section (1:7–6:15) presents reports of Zechariah's eight night visions. In these vision reports, the prophet announces various aspects of the coming age of salvation for Judah. These include announcing the building of the Temple and designating appointed leaders to the accomplishment of God's will throughout the world. The third section (Chapters 7–8) is a collection of various prophecies, beginning and ending with oracles concerning fasting.

The Book of Zechariah is both prophetic and priestly. He shares the conviction with the earlier prophets that he has received God's message for the people. He shares a concern for the Temple and its ritual with past and present priests. Above all, Zechariah is convinced that God is working in his time to bring in a religious kingdom that will have its center in Jerusalem.

❑ *Zechariah 1:1-6.* The initial verse is a superscription only to this first prophetic speech. The second year of Darius would have been 520 B.C. The eighth month would be in mid-October through mid-November. Zechariah began prophesying some two months after Haggai did. What is reported here as his first address serves to introduce the book. This speech is similar to the earlier prophets' reports of their calls. That is, Zechariah associates himself with his predecessors. He reminds the people that prophetic words, including his, are effective. The major point of the speech, however, is a summons to the people to return to God. They should acknowledge that God is active and will deal with people according to their deeds.

❏ *Zechariah 1:7-17.* The first of the night visions, reported by the prophet himself, follows verse 7. Zechariah describes what he saw and heard. The prophet asks what these figures are. First an angel responds. Then "the man standing among the myrtle trees" (verse 10) answers. He explains that they are the ones who patrol the earth for God. It then becomes increasingly difficult to identify the various participants in the vision. In any case, Zechariah hears an angel pleading with God to have mercy on Jerusalem—seventy years is enough to suffer (verse 12). The response, first by God and then by the angel, is an announcement of salvation to Jerusalem. The announcement includes the promise that the Temple will be rebuilt and the cities of Judah will prosper.

❏ *Zechariah 1:18-20.* The report of the second night vision is quite brief. But it contains the same major elements as the others (the description of the vision, the prophet's inquiry of an angelic interpreter, and the explanation of the meaning of the vision). Zechariah sees four horns. He is informed that they are the ones that scattered Judah and Jerusalem. He then sees four craftsmen (God's agents for destruction). He is informed that they have come to terrify and cast down the "horns of the nations who lifted up their horns against the land of Judah" (verse 20). The message of the vision is one of salvation to Judah and Jerusalem. The number four occurs frequently in prophetic and later apocalyptic vision reports.

❏ *Zechariah 2:1-13.* The third vision report is presented in verses 1-5. The report is followed by a prophetic speech. In the speech God calls for those who are scattered, particularly in Babylon, to return to Zion. In the vision the prophet sees a man with a measuring line in his hand. The man tells Zechariah he is measuring Jerusalem. When the angelic interpreter appears, another angel runs up and is told to announce that Jerusalem will be inhabited. God will be a wall of fire around her and the glory within her. Jerusalem will once again be rebuilt and inhabited by the exiles.

❏ *Zechariah 4:1-14.* The prophet receives the fifth vision like a person being awakened from sleep. He sees a lampstand with a bowl on top and seven lights, with seven channels to the lights. They are standing between two olive trees. He is informed that the vision is a message for Zerubbabel, the governor. The seven are "the eyes of the LORD, which range throughout the earth" (verse 10). The message is that Zerubbabel should rule not by might, but by God's Spirit (verse 6). The two trees stand for the "two who are anointed to serve the LORD" (verse 14), that is, Zerubbabel and Joshua, the high priest.

❑ *Zechariah 5:1-4.* In the sixth vision, Zechariah sees a flying scroll. The scroll is explained as the curse that goes through the whole world. It goes out to accuse the guilty and bring to them their due punishment.

❑ *Zechariah 5:5-11.* The focus of the seventh vision is a basket, or ephah. An ephah holds about five gallons. Inside is a woman identified as "wickedness." Two women with wings then carry the container of wickedness off to Babylonia (or Shinar). There a house will be built for it.

❑ *Zechariah 6:1-15.* The eighth and final vision (verses 1-8) is perhaps the most dramatic of all. This vision is a scene of four chariots appearing from between two mountains. Each chariot is drawn by horses of different colors. The angelic interpreter explains that once they have presented themselves before God they will go out to patrol the earth. Each will go to one of the four winds. The will of God will be established in all the world.

Added to the final vision report is an account of an action performed by the prophet upon instructions from God. Zechariah makes a crown, takes some of the exiles with him, and places the crown on the head of Joshua the high priest. He announces that Joshua is to build the Temple, bear royal honor, and rule. Royal messianic hopes and expectations are applied to the high priest.

❑ *Zechariah 7:1-7.* Here the prophet presents a revelation concerning fasts and mourning. This revelation comes two years later than the oracle given in 1:1.

Someone has a question about a regular day of mourning in the fifth month. That was the month the Temple was destroyed by the Babylonians (2 Kings 25:8-9). The mourning was probably for the loss of the Temple. Should such a practice continue once the Temple is rebuilt? In response, Zechariah criticizes the people for their attitude. Acts of devotion should be just that, and not for self-satisfaction.

❏ *Zechariah 7:8-14.* This sermon is on the theme of prophetic morality. Zechariah calls for justice in court, kindness, and mercy. He prohibits oppression of the widow, the orphan, the foreigner, and the poor. No one should plan evil against a brother. Because the people failed to follow such instructions in the law, they were carried into exile.

❏ *Zechariah 8:1-8.* The word of the Lord is an unqualified announcement of salvation. It promises that God will return to Zion and Jerusalem. Jerusalem will once again be called the faithful city, the holy mountain. Moreover, God will save all the people, bringing them back to that city. Verse 8 reiterates the ancient covenant. This time it is in reverse order—they will be my people and I will be their God.

❏ *Zechariah 8:9-17.* Zechariah calls for the Temple to be rebuilt. God will then deal generously with the people. Then he reminds them that God had punished their predecessors because of their sins. He calls for them to deal with one another justly as the proper response to God's grace.

❏ *Zechariah 8:18-23.* In the days to come, fasts shall become celebrations of joy and gladness. Furthermore, people from all over the world will come to the Temple in Jerusalem to seek God and God's favor. Jews will be the most respected of peoples because God is with them.

DIMENSION THREE:
WHAT DOES THE BIBLE MEAN TO ME?

Church and State

The Old Testament assumes a relationship between the state and religious institutions that is quite different from ours. Through most of ancient Israel's history, church and state coincided with each another. Religion was established by the state, and the state by the religious faith. Kings built and maintained temples, and ruled by the grace and election of God. The citizens were God's own covenant people.

A very different situation had arisen in the time of Zechariah. The old Israelite and Judean states no longer existed. The people lived in what had become a province of the Persian Empire. Religion and state were different. But the old ideas and hopes had not died. When the prophets of this era talked of "the anointed one," they expressed the hope that government and religion would once again be united. For all practical purposes, the reality was that what had been even more than a state religion had become a religion limited to the Temple. Political matters were determined from outside and quite apart from the faith of the people of Judea.

What are the advantages and disadvantages of each alternative? The Constitution of the United States, in order to preserve religious freedom, prohibits the "establishment" of a particular religion. That leaves us to struggle constantly with the question of the relation between religion and politics, between church and state. What are the dangers—for both church and state—if one religion determines the course of political affairs? What are the dangers—for both church and state—if men and women of faith who make up churches have no influence on the course of political affairs?

Rejoice greatly, O Daughter of Zion! /
Shout, Daughter of Jerusalem (9:9)!

—— 12 ——
God's Final Victory
Zechariah 9–14

DIMENSION ONE:
WHAT DOES THE BIBLE SAY?

Answer these questions by reading Zechariah 9

1. What will God do to Tyre? (9:3-4)

2. How does Zion's king come to the city of Jerusalem? (9:9)

3. How extensive will be the king of Zion's dominion? (9:10)

Answer these questions by reading Zechariah 10

4. Why do the people wander like sheep? (10:2)

5. At whom is God angry? (10:3)

6. When God signals for the people and brings them in, how many will there be? (10:8)

7. What will happen to Assyria and Egypt? (10:11)

Answer these questions by reading Zechariah 11

8. Why are the oaks of Bashan commanded to wail? (11:2)

9. What do those who sell the flock say? (11:5)

10. What did the shepherd of the flock marked for slaughter name the two staffs? (11:7)

11. What does the shepherd do to his staff? (11:10)

12. How much was God paid as wages by the sellers of the sheep? (11:12)

13. What did it mean that the second staff, Union, was broken? (11:14)

Answer these questions by reading Zechariah 12

14. What does God say Jerusalem will soon become? (12:2-3)

15. What will the leaders of Judah be like on that day? (12:6)

16. With whom will the feeblest of the inhabitants be compared on that day? (12:8)

17. What does the Lord promise to pour out on the house of David and the inhabitants of Jerusalem? (12:10)

Answer these questions by reading Zechariah 13

18. Why will the fountain be opened? (13:1)

19. What will God banish from the land? (13:2)

20. What will happen to the one-third from the whole land who shall be left alive? (13:8-9)

THE MINOR PROPHETS

21. What is to happen to the people when the nations gather against Jerusalem for battle? (14:2)

2. What will flow out of Jerusalem? (14:8)

23. What will happen to the peoples that fight against Jerusalem? (14:12)

24. What will the survivors among the nations do year after year? (14:16)

25. What is to be inscribed on the bells of the horses? (14:20)

DIMENSION TWO: WHAT DOES THE BIBLE MEAN?

These chapters contain a series of diverse prophetic addresses different from the speeches in Zechariah 1–8. Many scholars feel that their style, point of view, and historical allusions reflect an era later than the first eight chapters. Zechariah, Joshua the high priest, Zerubbabel the governor, and the problems of the construction of the Temple are not mentioned. But the Greeks who appeared in the Near East with the conquests of Alexander the Great in 344 B.C. are alluded to.

This collection has two main parts. Chapters 9–11 and 12–14. Each part is introduced by its own superscription. The first part begins with an announcement of judgment against other nations (9:1-8). It first welcomes the appearance of the Greeks and then condemns them (9:11-17). God is acting in and through historical events. The second part (Chapters 12–14) also announces that God is acting and will act. That action is viewed as a more dramatic transformation. The units in this section are more similar to the visions in the books of Daniel and Revelation.

❏ *Zechariah 9:1-8.* This prophetic announcement of the future has two parts. Verses 1-6a proclaim God's disaster for a series of foreign nations and cities. Verses 6b-8 promise God's protection to the people. The proclamation of disaster is directed against Syria (Hadrach, Damascus, Aram, and Hamath), Phoenicia (Tyre and Sidon), and four Philistine cities (Ashkelon, Gaza, Ekron, and Ashdod). While the announcement against the foreigners speaks of God in the third person, the assurance of protection to God's people is in the first person. God promises to encamp at the Temple and guard against any oppressors.

❏ *Zechariah 9:9-10.* This famous passage is quoted in Matthew 21:5 and John 12:15. The king is to ride only one animal. The last two lines of verse 9 are typical Hebrew parallelism. The coming king is to be triumphant and humble at the same time. He exercises dominion over all the world, but not through force. This coming king will destroy the instruments of war. The earliest Christians saw Jesus as the Messiah described here.

❏ *Zechariah 9:11-17.* These verses consist of three announcements of salvation for the people of God. Verses 11-13 promise that the prisoners will be set free and the sons of Zion will dominate the sons of Greece. Verses 14-15 announce that God will lead the people into a victorious battle. Verses 16-17 describe the new day when God will care for the flock.

❏ *Zechariah 10:1-2.* The main concern of these lines is idolatry in several forms. The people must pray only to God. God makes the storm clouds, gives the rain, and provides the vegetation. Next is an attack upon idols, diviners, and dreamers. Apparently the people have either prayed to or consulted such figures. The message of the prophet is that they must rely only on God.

❏ *Zechariah 10:3-12.* This speech of the Lord begins by expressing God's anger against the shepherds. It then announces that God will care for the flock. The shepherds probably represent some particular leaders of the community. Verses 3-5 in particular must reflect a disagreement in the community over its leadership. The specific problem cannot be determined, though. It may have concerned the priesthood and the high priest. In any case, God disapproved of those who were in charge.

❏ *Zechariah 11:1-3.* The prophet announces the destruction of the majestic forests. The announcement is in the form of a taunt against the forests. The speaker probably does not refer to the literal destruction of the trees. The language is metaphorical. The cedars of Lebanon, the oaks of Bashan, and the lions probably stand for major world powers or their kings.

❏ *Zechariah 11:4-17.* God commands the prophet to perform a series of symbolic actions. The prophet acted as shepherd of "the flock marked for slaughter," conveying the message of judgment. He took two staffs, naming them Favor and Union. He tended the sheep, and then destroyed three shepherds. Next he broke the staff called Favor, indicating that the covenant was ended. Taking his pay of thirty pieces of silver, he cast it into the treasury. He broke the second staff Union. This indicates that the brotherhood between Israel and Judah was annulled. Finally, God commands him to take the tools of "a foolish shepherd" again. God is raising up a shepherd who does not care for his sheep, but instead only destroys.

Unlike the remainder of the book, this passage is an announcement of judgment against the leaders and apparently also against the people. The reference to the thirty pieces of silver is quoted in Matthew 27:9-10, where it is attributed to Jeremiah.

❏ *Zechariah 12:1–13:6.* This section, composed of five or six announcements that originally were independent, has a unity of theme and style. The common theme announces the day of the Lord ("on that day"). Those in Judah and Jerusalem in the last days before God's final victory will be especially troubled.

As in later apocalyptic literature such as Daniel and Revelation, the end time is seen as a period of trial and tribulation for the people of God. But the triumph of God will be worldwide.

Zechariah 12:1-9 concerns a great siege against Jerusalem. The images of Jerusalem as "a cup that sends all the surrounding peoples reeling" and an "immovable rock" appear in verses 1-5. Those who come up to besiege Jerusalem will regret that they have done so. Verse 6 announces that the clans of Judah will become instruments of God's war against those who come up against Jerusalem. According to verses 7-9, first Judah will be victorious, and then the house of David, as the Lord protects Jerusalem.

In 12:10-14 the writer announces a time when God will pour out a spirit of compassion on the house of David and the inhabitants of Jerusalem. A period of mourning will also occur. Determining who the mourning is for is not possible. They are mourning for someone whom "they have pierced." The Gospel of John takes this image as a prophecy of the death of Jesus (John 19:34-37).

The first verse of Chapter 13 announces a cleansing fountain for the house of David and the people of Jerusalem. Verses 2-6 promise that idols, prophets, and the spirit of impurity shall be removed from the land. How could a prophet see such an event as good news? Either these lines are speaking of false prophets, or they look forward to a time when God will communicate directly with the people and will not need to speak through prophets.

❑ *Zechariah 13:7-9.* The judgment against the shepherd and the sheep will be a cleansing judgment. Two thirds of the people will perish. One third will be refined as silver and gold. For a very similar understanding of the purpose of divine judgment see Isaiah 1:18-26.

❑ *Zechariah 14:1-5.* As in Chapter 12, these verses announce a day of battle with Jerusalem in the center. Unlike Chapter 12, however, God brings up the enemies and allows them to capture the city and carry off half of the people. But then the Lord fights against those same nations. When God appears, nature is transformed.

❑ *Zechariah 14:6-15.* The theme of nature's transformation in the final days is continued in a series of oracles. God alone will reign over the entire earth (verse 9). Jerusalem will be elevated over the earth and inhabited (verses 9-11). God will bring a terrible plague on those who fight against Jerusalem, throwing them into a panic (verses 12-15).

❑ *Zechariah 14:16-21.* All those among the nations who survive the great day of battle will come as pilgrims to Jerusalem to worship God. Given the time and circumstances of the prophet, the last lines (verses 20-21) are perhaps the most dramatic announcement of all. In a time that emphasizes the importance of ritual purity, he announces that even ordinary cooking pots will be as sacred as the bowls of the altar. All of life, in other words, will be sacred to God.

DIMENSION THREE:
WHAT DOES THE BIBLE MEAN TO ME?

The New Testament Meaning of the Old Testament

We have seen some of the passages in Zechariah 9–14 that are cited in the New Testament. The account of Jesus' triumphant entry into Jerusalem quotes Zechariah 9:9. The report of Judas's wages uses Zechariah 11:12-13. John's account of the death of Jesus quotes Zechariah 12:10. And many other direct and indirect New Testament quotations appear in Zechariah. The New Testament writers often interpreted events in the life of Jesus as fulfillments of ancient prophecies. These writers took for granted that the ancient Jewish Scriptures were true and authoritative. What had to be argued and proven was the validity of the new message that Jesus Christ was the Messiah. Thus Paul, citing an early Christian creed, emphasizes that what happened in Jesus was "according to the Scriptures" (1 Corinthians 15:3-4).

As we study the Old Testament prophets, we often recognize that their words, including some that the New Testament writers apply to Jesus, referred to persons and events in their own times. How do we come to terms with the fact that many texts have both an Old Testament and a New Testament meaning? Must we choose between them, accepting the one and rejecting the other? Must we impose the New Testament interpretation upon the Old Testament passages, or vice versa?

The fact that the Old Testament forms part of Christian Scripture indicates that it should be taken with utmost seriousness on its own terms and in its own historical context. We recognize that of a great many messianic expectations and prophecies, only some finally apply to Jesus. The ancient prophets would not have had Jesus Christ in mind, though their words helped to prepare the way for his coming. Furthermore, often their prophecies meant more than they knew or intended. That idea in itself is not unusual. All important written expressions take new meanings and a life of their own as they are read by different people in new and later situations.

Thus, when the earliest Christians were trying to make sense of the dramatic events that had happened in their time, they often found that the words of the ancient prophets actually expressed what they had experienced. The suffering redeemer actually had been expected long before he came. Now they knew that his name was Jesus, and through him God meant to establish that universal reign.

See, I will send my messenger, who will
prepare the way before me (3:1).

— 13 —
The Messenger of the Lord
Malachi

DIMENSION ONE:
WHAT DOES THE BIBLE SAY?

Answer these questions by reading Malachi 1

1. What does God tell Israel? (1:2)

2. What will God do if the people of Edom say they will rebuild their ruins? (1:4)

3. What does God ask the priests? (1:6)

4. What does the passage say about God's name? (1:11)

5. What do priests bring to the altar? (1:13)

6. What does the Lord curse? (1:14)

Answer these questions by reading Malachi 2

7. For whom is the Lord's command? (2:1)

8. What will happen if the priests do not honor God's name? (2:2)

9. With whom did God make a covenant of life and peace? (2:4-5)

10. What should the people do? (2:7)

11. How has Judah committed a detestable thing in Israel and Jerusalem? (2:11)

12. What has the one God done? (2:15)

13. How have the people wearied God with their words? (2:17)

Answer these questions by reading Malachi 3

14. Who is God sending, and why? (3:1)

15. What is the messenger to do? (3:3)

16. What does God promise to do if the people return? (3:7)

17. How are the people robbing God? (3:8)

18. What does God tell the people to do, and why? (3:10)

19. What will happen when the Lord blesses the people? (3:12)

20. How have the people spoken against the Lord? (3:13-15)

21. What was written when those who feared God talked with one another and God heard them? (3:16)

22. What will happen to all the arrogant and all evildoers? (4:1)

23. What will be the fate of those who revere the name of the Lord? (4:2-3)

24. What are the people told to remember? (4:4)

25. What will Elijah do before the great and dreadful day comes? (4:6)

DIMENSION TWO: WHAT DOES THE BIBLE MEAN?

❏ *Malachi 1:1.* The superscription to the book includes the title ("An oracle: The word of the LORD"), the addresses ("to Israel"), and the name of the author ("through Malachi"). However, *Malachi* is probably not a proper name but a title. It means "my messenger," as indicated by 3:1. Malachi is identified with the messenger who would come to prepare the way for the day of the Lord.

❏ *Malachi 1:2-5.* These verses are a dialogue in which only one party actually speaks. The speaker quotes the words of the people being spoken to. The dialogue here is a prophetic speech in which God addresses Israel. The people ask God, "How have you loved us?" The response is that God loved Jacob (that is, Israel) but hated his brother Esau (that is, Edom). God shows this love for the former by judging the latter. Behind

THE MINOR PROPHETS

this idea is the hatred between Judah and Edom after the Babylonian conquest. Edom took part of Judah's territory then.

❏ *Malachi 1:6–2:9.* This unit develops a dialogue between God and the priests. But it also concerns the laity. The dialogue contains two major elements. One element is the indictment of the priests (1:6-14). The laity are also indicted for making inadequate sacrifices. The other element is a sermonic paragraph calling for change and including threats and promises (2:1-9).

The debate begins when the prophet accuses the priests of dishonoring God. When the priests ask how they have dishonored God, the indictment is spelled out (verses 7-8). The prophet assumes the people are violating known requirements concerning sacrificial animals. God vows not to accept such offerings, but affirms the greatness of the Lord's name (1:10-11). God curses the person who vowed a perfect male animal from his flock yet sacrifices one that is blemished (1:14).

The prophet turns from indictment to call for change. He emphasizes the curse that will come into effect if the priests do not heed God's command (2:2-3). God reminds the priests of the blessing that had been theirs. This blessing will probably continue if they change (2:4-6). God then reminds the priests that they are messengers of God. They are responsible for knowledge and instruction, but have caused many to go astray (2:7-8). Finally, the priests, and with them the people, are despised and in trouble because they have not followed God's way (2:9).

❏ *Malachi 2:10-16.* This debate concerns men who divorce their Israelite wives to marry foreigners. The questions (verse 10a) stress the solidarity of the covenant people as children of one God. Then an accusing question points out that being faithless to one another violates the covenant with God. The problem is not so much the fact that the wives are foreign, but that they pay allegiance to foreign gods. If Malachi is narrow and restrictive, it is for religious rather than nationalistic reasons.

Now (verses 13-16) the prophet takes the side of the divorced wives. Though the husbands pray and bring offerings,

God does not respond to them because they have abandoned the wives of their youth. Here the word *covenant* is used in another way. It does not define the relationship between God and Israel. The word is used to characterize marriage. God sanctified that covenant as a witness and hates divorce.

❏ *Malachi 2:17–3:5.* Here the prophet turns to another group within Israel. He might have had in mind the attitudes of the people as a whole. The opponents in the debate are those who question the justice of God. They have wearied God by saying two things. First, they say, "All who do evil are good in the eyes of the LORD." That statement implies that God either does not know the difference between good and evil or that God prefers evil. Their second question is the same as saying that there is no God of justice. The answer to these questions is given in the form of an announcement of the day of the Lord's judgment (3:1-5). A time is coming when the God of justice will act to establish that justice in the world. The prophet has two stages in the divine drama in mind. First, God will send a messenger to prepare the way (3:1-4). This prophecy was applied to John the Baptist. Second, God will come in judgment against all those who are not obedient to the laws (3:5).

❏ *Malachi 3:6-12.* These verses are addressed to the people as a whole. They return to the theme of Malachi 1:6–2:9, appropriate sacrifices and offerings. Accusations of faithlessness are coupled with admonitions and exhortations to return to God.

❏ *Malachi 3:13–4:3.* This section is similar to 2:17–3:5. God accuses some of speaking falsely by saying that it is vain to serve God. They question the value of worship. They assert that evildoers prosper (verses 13-15). Then follows a report that some of the people feared God, and their names were written in a "scroll of remembrance" (verse 16). God then announces that a day will come when all things will be set right (3:17–4:3). Then God will reward the faithful and destroy all evildoers.

❏ *Malachi 4:4-5.* Two short units conclude the book. The first (verse 4) is an admonition to heed the law of Moses. Verse 5 picks up the theme of the messenger who will prepare the way for the coming of the Lord (3:1-4). Elijah is thought to be the messenger whose primary function will be to bring about repentance.

DIMENSION THREE:
WHAT DOES THE BIBLE MEAN TO ME?

Issues in Malachi

The Book of Malachi raises a great many issues that contemporary Christians also face. A central theme of the book is the importance of proper worship. In his time, the prophet understood such worship primarily in terms of appropriate sacrifices and offerings. He criticizes those who bring less than perfect animals to offer and those who fail to pay their tithes. The sacredness of the Temple and the altar should be maintained. Both people and priests should be scrupulous and dedicated. How do these concerns relate to our own worship?

A second issue, directly related to this first one, concerns the rewards of faithfulness. This prophet seems to draw an almost direct relationship between faithfulness and prosperity. If people pay their tithes, then the fields will flourish (Malachi 3:10-12). Is that view consistent with the message of the New Testament? Is it consistent with human experience? Why, or why not?

A third question involves the issue of the justice of God. In response to those who assert that evildoers prosper (Malachi 3:15; 2:17), the prophet announces a coming day of the Lord when all persons will get what they deserve. How is that response related to the perspective stated elsewhere, that the righteous will prosper immediately?

A fourth set of issues concerns human relationships. The prophet repeats the ancient prophetic concerns with social justice, especially the responsibility of the people for the weak and powerless (Malachi 3:5). He expresses a particular concern for faithfulness in marriage. He presents one of the strongest biblical statements against divorce (2:16). Behind that particular concern is his opposition to the Israelite practice of marrying foreigners. He is not so much concerned with purity of race as with purity of religion. Does he express the narrow views opposed with the Book of Jonah?

CPSIA information can be obtained
at www.ICGtesting.com
Printed in the USA
LVOW13s0044260517

535810LV00007B/31/P